W9-AYO-173

Julius
Caesar

JULIUS CAESAR

JOHN GUNTHER

Illustrated by
JOSEPH CELLINI

RANDOM HOUSE · NEW YORK

(handwritten, left margin) Dec Wing 12/31/59 1.95

3449

81670

(stamp) EAU CLAIRE PUBLIC LIBRARY

First Printing

© Copyright, 1959, by John Gunther

All rights reserved under International and Pan-American Copyright
Conventions. Published in New York by Random House, Inc., and
simultaneously in Toronto, Canada, by Random House of Canada, Limited.

Library of Congress Catalog Card Number: 59–10971
Manufactured in the United States of America by
H. Wolff, New York

This Book is
Dedicated with Love and Thanks
to
ALEXANDER and TATIANA LIBERMAN

Villa Va-et-Vient
Ste. Maxime.

Contents

PART ONE

I	Caesar and the Pirates	3
II	In Those Days Rome Was Like This . . .	9
III	Family Background	15
IV	The Youth of Caesar	23
V	Out in the East	34
VI	How Rome Was Ruled—the Senate and the People	40
VII	The Political Arena	47
VIII	Caesar Struggles to Get Ahead	55
IX	Pompey, Crassus, and the Triumvirate	63

PART TWO

X	Caesar Conquers Gaul	77
XI	He Has Interests in Rome, Too, While Fighting a Thousand Miles Away	89

XII   The Last Act in Gaul   103
XIII   The Rubicon   111

PART THREE

XIV   The Civil War   121
XV   Cleopatra—and After   130
XVI   Battles in Africa and Spain   138
XVII   Back in Rome   146
XVIII The Ides of March   158
XIX   Aftermath   169
       Bibliography   175
       Index   177

PART I

❧ I ❧

Caesar and the Pirates

When Gaius Julius Caesar was still in his twenties he took a trip to Rhodes, an island in the Aegean Sea. This was long before he was well known outside his own circle. Nobody knew that this young man was going to become master of the world some day. He was a youth of good family, something of a spendthrift and gambler, eager to get ahead in politics and war, but still untried. Few Romans had ever heard of him.

The youthful Caesar had been trying to make a name for himself in the law courts. He had just fought two interesting cases, and had lost them both. Now he determined to gain something out of these defeats. He was a resolute as well as brilliant young man, who never missed an opportunity to improve himself. There was no false pride in Caesar.

So he decided to leave Italy and go out to Rhodes. Here lived a famous teacher of language, law, and oratory named Apollonius Molo. Caesar's idea was to spend the winter studying with Molo, so that he would lose no more cases, and also get a rest from Rome.

Near a small islet Caesar and his companions were captured by a gang of pirates. The Mediterranean was infested with bloodthirsty pirates in those days.

The pirate chieftain saw from Caesar's clothes and manner that this was a young man of the Roman aristocracy, probably with rich and influential friends. The pirate said, "We are going to hold you for a ransom of twenty talents." This was a very large sum for the time, about $20,000. "Pay us twenty talents, or we will strangle you and cast your body into the sea."

Caesar replied, "What? Only twenty talents? You are ignorant pirates, and do not know what a prize you have."

The pirates stared at him, astonished.

Without a tremor and showing his full contempt for these wretched barbarians, Caesar continued with calm effrontery, "I am worth fifty talents. That will be the amount of my ransom, not a miserable twenty!"

Caesar sent several of his companions to the nearby port of Miletus to borrow this vast sum of money, and prepared to make the best possible use of his captivity.

The pirates kept him prisoner for thirty-eight days and treated him well. Not only were they impressed by his bold confidence and easy manner; they also grew to like him. In fact, before many days had passed, it was Caesar who seemed to be the captor of these pirates rather than the reverse. As one old chronicler says, they waited upon him as upon a prince.

"You disturb my sleep," Caesar complained. "Your rude games go on too long at night. Pray move your camp further from my bed," he commanded.

The pirates did so.

Caesar taught the pirates Roman games of skill and chance, encouraged them to take regular exercise, as he himself always did, and became quite fond of them. At the same time, he insulted them without interruption, calling them stupid blockheads. Moreover, he was perfectly frank about what he intended to do with them once he was free. He said candidly, "The minute I am a free man I shall return here, take you in battle, and crucify you, every man!"

The pirates did not take this threat seriously,

and went on with their games and drinking. They thought that Caesar was simple-minded, made bold by youth.

Caesar, who from his earliest days had been interested in literary composition, occupied himself comfortably with writing verse and practicing oratory on the pirates. He would gather them around him at dusk, and make resounding political speeches as if he were at home in the Roman Forum.

Presently Caesar's associates returned with the fifty talents, having succeeded in borrowing the sum from various moneylenders. Caesar paid over the money, saluted the ragamuffin pirates, and warned them once more, "It will not be long before you will see me again. And I shall crucify every one of you!"

Caesar and his men set sail.

He landed at Miletus, borrowed more money, and equipped a small naval task force. Promptly he returned to the island of the pirates, seized them, and brought them to the city of Pergamum. Then he notified the Roman governor there that he had captured a dangerous gang of pirates and had committed them to prison. "Deal with them," Caesar said. "They are your responsibility."

But the governor hesitated and delayed. He

thought he might make a lot of money out of the pirates by selling them to somebody else, so he did not condemn them to death.

Caesar went to the prison himself, hauled the pirates out of their cells, and duly had them crucified. But crucifixion is the most cruel of all deaths, and Caesar mercifully saw to it that the pirates' throats were cut beforehand.

This anecdote tells a good deal about Caesar. All men are riddles, and Caesar more than most; but already in his youth certain lines in his character were strongly sketched out. He was confident, fixed in will, and, so far as it was possible to be, just. Three things above all distinguished him his whole life long: He had absolute courage, ambition, and a serious mind.

❦ II ❦

In Those Days Rome Was Like This . . .

Caesar's most obvious accomplishment was that he unified almost the whole of the known ancient world, after conquering a great deal of it. More than this, he helped transform this immense area, populated by hundreds of different peoples, into an empire which in one form or other lasted for almost fifteen hundred years.

He spread Rome out so that it covered most of the earth. He was much more than a brilliant military chieftain, more than a mere soldier, although he was one of the greatest soldiers who ever lived. Caesar was a true statesman, with tremendous far-seeing energy and vision. People everywhere adopted the Roman pattern, or had it imposed on them. Rome became the "Eternal City."

History has never quite got over Caesar. It has

been truly said of him that he was the first
modern man, and his impact was so great that
two thousand years after his death he still seems
to be alive.

Before telling the wonderful story of Caesar's
life and works we must go back a bit and describe
something of the background of Rome itself, its
heritage and institutions.

Rome in Caesar's day was the most up-and-
coming as well as powerful city in the world. A
citizen of Rome had special distinction everywhere. Moreover, the Romans were a sturdy, in-
dependent-minded folk, and every Roman felt tra-
ditionally that he was the equal of every other
Roman. The fact that Rome had such a special
status helped to make Caesar's conquests possible.
The Romans felt that it was their destiny, even
their duty, to be rulers of the earth.

But while Rome was the greatest city in the
world, it was also an extremely small town in
some respects. Everybody in the upper circles
knew everybody else, and rule was concentrated
in a clique of a hundred or so leading families,
most of which were related to the others.

Caesar belonged to one of the most distinguished
of the old Roman families, and this was an important
asset to his career.

And where did these old Roman families come from? What was the origin of Rome itself?

Well, more than a thousand years earlier, tribes of Indo-European people flooded down into the Italian peninsula from their original homelands north of the Alps. One group of these came to be known as Latins. They were a primitive folk who lived by cultivating small plots of land. Their first settlement was called Latium and was situated near the river Tiber in central Italy. The word "Latin" comes from "Latium."

To the north were a warlike people, the Etruscans. In the south Greek colonies began to develop, and flourishing Greek settlements arose in southern Italy and Sicily. Beautiful Greek temples may be seen in these areas to this day.

The early Latins made their position firm, began to spread out, and soon built up a brisk trade with their neighbors. The most convenient trading post for everybody lay on the Tiber at a point where seven small hills commanded a portage. Here a cluster of villages grew up, and eventually this became the city of Rome.

Everyone is familiar with the legend that the actual founders of Rome were two youthful brothers, Romulus and Remus. The date is supposed to have been 753 B.C. Romulus and Remus were victims of an evil king, who left them to die on the banks of the Tiber. He did this in order to pass the throne down to his own branch of the family. But the infant boys were rescued by a she-wolf, who suckled them, and years later Romulus became the king. The she-wolf has been a symbol of Rome ever since.

Probably no such person as Romulus ever really lived, but, interestingly enough, Caesar's family claimed descent from him as well as from the goddess Venus. Also Romulus was supposed to have been descended from Mars, the god of war. So Caesar could claim both royal and divine lineage.

Rome was a kingdom in its early years. Several of its kings were Etruscans. The Roman citizenry came to resent their rule, which was cruel and greedy, and eventually threw them out. In 509 B.C. Rome became a free man's republic, a city state. The Romans hated kingship and the repressive rule that monarchy was apt to bring. They wanted their leaders to be elected men of the people, so that they could govern themselves.

The early Roman republic spread out and prospered. The city had a central geographical position and an intensely virile citizenry. Yet Rome had troubles. For instance, a fierce people known

as the Gauls, barbarians from the north, were a perpetual menace. In 390 B.C. the Gauls even succeeded in penetrating far south into Italy and sacking Rome.

By 264 B.C., despite the Gauls, Rome was the master of all Italy up to the Po Valley. But the outward thrust of the tough, able Romans brought conflict with Carthage, a powerful rival republic on the northern coast of Africa, across the Mediterranean. Three tremendous wars, known as the Punic Wars, had to be fought before Carthage was finally beaten and destroyed. Then the Romans spread out into Greece and Asia Minor.

Nothing, it seemed, could stop these ambitious and energetic people. By 133 B.C. Rome commanded almost the whole of the Mediterranean, including a large part of Spain, and was the foremost military and commercial power in the world.

Thus, Caesar inherited a lively and robust tradition. Roman history was, and still is, studded with heroic memories. Most of the old legends stressed two things—patriotism and a stoic willingness to suffer if suffering was necessary.

The Romans, in Caesar's day, were highly civilized in some respects, and not at all civilized in others. They did not produce poets and dramatists and philosophers on the level of the Greeks, and much of their play was abominably cruel. They went in for gladiatorial "games," and threw prisoners to wild beasts.

But the Romans were great builders, great engineers. They had practical minds and were efficient businessmen. They believed in law, good citizenship, and order. Above all they developed an extremely interesting political system, the roots of which survive in many governments today.

When Caesar came to power Rome was, in theory, still supposed to be a self-governing democracy. But ominous signs of change had come.

❧ III ❧

Family Background

Probably Gaius Julius Caesar was born in 102 B.C., but nobody knows the exact date and historians still argue about it. If the year 102 is correct Caesar was only fifty-eight years old when he was assassinated in 44 B.C.—cut off in his prime. If he had lived even a few years more, there is no telling what further soaring contribution he might have made to the life of Rome and the civilization that has derived from Rome all over the world. He died just as his most mature work was beginning.

Caesar rose out of the great Julian family. This was not merely an ancient family, but also a very distinguished one. For generations various Julians had been among the leading men of Rome. Caesar had several uncles and cousins who were consuls or who occupied other high positions of state, and the whole family was marked by its devotion to public service.

The actual name "Caesar," which was the surname of the Julian family, is obscure in origin. Literally it means "curly." But also it had an odd meaning—"elephant"—in the language of Carthage. Carthage, as we know, had been ruthlessly destroyed by the might of Rome half a century before Caesar was born. But Carthaginian influence was strong in Rome for a long period, and it is possible that the Roman Caesars first picked up their name from Carthage, which was famous for its fighting elephants.

Caesar's father was named Lucius. Little is known about him. Like all Roman heads of a family, he ruled his wife and children with absolute authority, but he seems to have been a kindly man. He was an aristocrat and a worthy citizen, but he never amounted to much. There is no record of what young Gaius thought of him, or vice versa. He died of a heart attack, while stooping to put on his sandals, when his son was sixteen.

Aurelia, Caesar's mother, was a more important influence. She was an "honest gentlewoman," devoted to her son and eager for his well-being. She taught him the classic Roman virtues—manliness, obedience, dignity, and the capacity to withstand pain without flinching. She knew that he would go far and, luckily, lived long enough to see his career magnificently launched.

Caesar was an only son. He had two sisters, but they play very little part in his story. One of them, however, has a claim to fame in that, years later, she was the grandmother of a young man named Octavius. He was Caesar's grandnephew and only surviving relative, and became his eventual successor. History knows him well under the name of Augustus Caesar, the first Emperor of Rome.

Now it is important to explain that Julius Caesar's family, the great Julian clan with its roots in the heroic past, was *patrician*. The patricians were not merely members of the aristocracy from a social point of view, but something more. They had a monopoly of political office in Rome for generations, and they dominated the Senate, which was the most powerful instrument of the Roman state.

On the other side were the plebs, or *plebeians*. The word means "multitude." The plebs were the common people—the mass of ordinary citizens who were the merchants, traders, soldiers, yeoman farmers, and middle class.

For a long time the chief issue in Rome was

the struggle between the ruling patricians and the
rising plebs. The plebs wanted their fair share of
power, and fought to get it. Gradually two political parties emerged—the Optimates, representing
the patricians, and the Populares, representing the
plebeians and the man in the street.

Optimates in the Senate were, speaking broadly,
the sticklers for constitutional rights, tradition, and
the old order. The Populares were the party of the
people, the radicals, the reformers.

By the time Caesar was born the plebs had
won a great deal, and the distinction between
patrician and pleb was thinning down. Even so,
the two political parties were fierce rivals, and
tension was acute.

Another word on background. For some time
Rome had been degenerating, and the old Roman
virtues declined. Citizens lost their stalwart standards. As the empire spread out and got rich, the
national character became corrupt. Discipline was
lax, and morality broke down. Stoicism, austerity,
and simple living gave way to extravagance and
slipshod manners.

Speculators and profiteers flourished. The newly
rich landowners squeezed out the peasants on the
farms until the whole country rocked with dis-

content. It seemed that the very life of the republic might be in danger.

Several great military leaders now rose out of this confusion and sought to gain power for themselves. Their pretext was that they were saving Rome from destruction. But, in order to make their rule strong enough, they had to become dictators, and thus they played havoc with the splendid old democratic tradition.

The first of these strong, willful men who seized supreme power was an astounding character named Marius. He was a plebeian, born of an illiterate peasant family. He broke all precedent by becoming consul over and over again. There was no doubt about his military prowess. He saved Rome from an onslaught of barbarians from the north, won other brilliant campaigns, and transformed the Roman army from a volunteer militia into a modern, professional fighting force.

Marius was crude, tough as oak, and violent. But from first to last he was a people's man, devoted to the people's interest. He despised the old aristocrats in the Senate, the corrupt moneylenders in the towns, and the landowners who were ruining the helpless peasantry. He was merciless to his enemies, and ruled—in part at least—by terror.

Now, Julius Caesar had an aunt named Julia. Probably she was the most important person in all his early upbringing. This was because she split away from the patrician heritage of the Julian family, and married none other than this extraordinary plebeian, Marius! This was a very unorthodox thing to do.

Caesar was born just after Marius won his first great battle against the Gauls, and he was only two years old when Marius became consul for the sixth time. But the towering figure of his Uncle Marius dominated all of his boyhood and early youth and had a profound influence on him.

Thus the youthful Caesar combined two strains in his person. He was a patrician of the most

exalted rank; but also he was a nephew of the rough plebeian dictator. He was an aristocrat of aristocrats; and also a man of the people, who had the blessing of the great Marius. He was on top; and also could derive power from the bottom.

Such a combination is rare in political history, and young Caesar made extremely good use of it, as we shall see.

❦ IV ❦

The Youth of Caesar

Although Caesar's family was old, patrician, and distinguished, the Caesars were not particularly well off. In fact, their fortune had shrunk almost to nothing when Caesar was a boy. Times had changed, and many aristocratic families had lost their wealth.

Caesar's mother and father lived in a suburban district of Rome that was not at all fashionable. Their house was modest, and their neighbors were artisans and people of small means. Caesar learned the value of money early, and for many years was acutely preoccupied by money problems.

Not much is known about Caesar's early years. There are no romantic stories about him, and he had no exceptional experiences as a boy. If he ever tamed a wild horse as Alexander the Great tamed Bucephalus, we do not know about it.

Most Roman boys of Caesar's class did not go to school but had tutors at home. Caesar was no exception. His tutor, oddly enough, was not a Roman but a native of Cisalpine Gaul—that is, northern Italy.

Caesar's tutor was named Antonius Gnipho. He was an exceptionally good teacher. Caesar learned Greek well, and was grateful to Gnipho all his life for opening up to him the wonders of Greek culture. Also Gnipho gave him the foundation of his mastery of a sound Latin style. Caesar learned to write Latin with clarity, simplicity, and force.

Caesar had a natural aptitude for study. He was sensible enough to be dutiful, and he always liked intellectual pursuits. For a time he thought of devoting his life to literature, and wrote numerous youthful poems and plays. Unfortunately, none of Caesar's early writing has survived. When his grand-nephew Augustus became Emperor he ordered all of Caesar's boyhood literary work to be destroyed, because he did not think that it would be good for his reputation.

Caesar was not particularly strong as a boy, and preferred books to games. But every Roman youngster in those days was expected to show athletic ability, and Caesar became a good runner, fencer, and horseman. His body was slight, but he trained it well. Later he became capable of feats of physical toughness and endurance that would have astonished his early playmates.

Even so, his health was a bit frail. He became somewhat deaf at a comparatively early age and, after he was thirty, suffered occasionally from fits of epilepsy. These attacks, however, could not have been very pronounced. They certainly never interfered with what work he had in hand.

Caesar grew to be about five feet eight. He was pale for an Italian. Even as a boy he was extraordinarily handsome, and maturity carved his features into the mold well known from sculpture that has come down to us. He had wonderfully luminous eyes, a nose classically arched and aquiline, and a mouth at once sensitive and firm. His face was that of both poet and commander.

He was always proud of his looks, and as a youth was vain—almost a dandy. He wore his hair with unconventional fanciness, and dressed in an individual style. His enemies called him effeminate, and on one occasion a gruff old chieftain dismissed him with the words, "That boy in petticoats!" The old chieftain, years later, would have been astonished to see how this "boy in petticoats" could win the hardest battles.

Caesar became bald in his later years, and was sensitive about this. Toward the end of his career he liked to wear the laurel crown which the Roman Senate had bestowed on him. Such a crown helped to conceal his baldness.

Most of Caesar's character traits were formed early. He was full of common sense, shrewdness, and realism. He had great natural courtesy, and, for all his ego, was almost always modest in his conduct. He was prudent, but, when he wanted to be, bold beyond the wildest dreams.

Roman boys matured early, and Caesar became of age when he was sixteen. At a ceremonial family gathering he was given the toga which symbolized manhood. Proudly he put it on.

Almost at once he got his first job. This came about through the influence of his Uncle Marius, who called the graceful boy to him and announced that he was to be a Priest of Jupiter.

In those days Rome still worshipped the traditional gods of classic times—Jupiter, Juno, Mars, Venus, Mercury, and so on. Much elaborate ritual was attached to this worship, and deserving young people were, as a result, given ceremonial posts in various religious institutions.

One of Caesar's functions, as Priest of Jupiter, was to be a junior clerk to the famous group of

ladies known as the Vestal Virgins. These were
women high in Roman society who were pledged
to chastity and who served the goddess Vesta.
Every Roman home had a hearth, which was the
center of all family festivity and which symbolized
the virtue and unity of the home. Vesta was the
goddess who protected the home and its hearth,
and the Vestal Virgins were her sacred representatives for this purpose.

Caesar, although only a boy, got along well
with the Vestal Virgins. He behaved toward them
with scrupulous respect, and they appreciated this
and liked him.

Now it came time for Caesar to get married, for
Roman youths and girls married early in those days.
His father arranged a match for him with a young
lady named Cossutia. Caesar did not like the idea
very much. Already this young man had a strong
and peppery will of his own. But out of filial regard for his father he consented to marry her. The
marriage did not, however, last more than a few
months, and a divorce followed. A little later Caesar's
father died.

Then when he was nineteen Caesar fell deeply
in love with a girl named Cornelia. She was fascinated by the brilliant young aristocrat, and agreed
to marry him. So she became his second wife, and

never ceased to love him. Soon they had a daughter, whom they named Julia.

Out of this match came the first great crisis of
Caesar's career. In fact his marriage to Cornelia
came near to costing him his life. This was be-
cause Cornelia was the daughter of a man named
Cinna, and a violent political crisis was shaking
Rome at just this time.

Again we must go back a bit. Marius was still
the most important personage in the state, but he
was getting old and had begun to lose his grip.
His fellow consul, who hoped to carry on his rule,
was Cinna. Thus Caesar, even more than before,
was closely associated with the Marius party. He
was not only Marius' nephew but the son-in-law
of Marius' chief henchman, Cinna.

A new figure had now arisen, Sulla. Sulla was a
monster. Also he was an extremely accomplished and
successful soldier and leader of men. He was the
opposite of Marius in most respects. He was fantastically dissolute, even for the Rome of that day,
and had a face that looked like a white sponge
blotched with purple. More important, in strict
contrast to the plebeian Marius, he was an aristocrat and a patrician who stood wholeheartedly on
the side of the Optimates and the reactionaries in
the Senate.

Conflict between Marius and Sulla brought civil war, and Sulla took Rome by force of arms. Marius died in 86 B.C. Then Sulla spent some years fighting in Greece and Asia. He returned to Rome in triumph, made himself dictator, and in 82 B.C., the year of Caesar's marriage, began to wreak a terrible vengeance on his enemies. He "proscribed" people—that is, ordered them slain without any trial or process of law. More than 5,000 stout Romans, including almost the entire leadership of the Populare party, died in the Sulla blood bath.

The grisly turmoil died down after a while. Sulla, looking about him warily, sought to make his position solid. He fixed his attention on affairs at every level, no matter how minor or personal. And his eye fell on Caesar.

Now Caesar had done no wrong. But he was obviously a coming young man, talented and ambitious. He was a people's man, the nephew of Marius and the son-in-law of Cinna, who had been killed. Sulla decided that he must be taught a lesson, so that he would know where authority now lay. He summoned Caesar to the Forum, the seat of the Roman government, and rebuked him sternly. Then he ordered him forthwith to divorce Cornelia.

This Caesar refused to do.

Such open defiance of the dictator, Sulla, was unprecedented and spectacular. Men had died for much less. But Caesar loved his young wife, and would not give her up.

Sulla decided, after an ugly pause, to be merciful. He did not order Caesar to be thrown into a dungeon or beheaded on the spot. Instead he dismissed him from his post as Priest of Jupiter, and ordered all of his property to be confiscated, together with Cornelia's. Then he ordered Caesar to leave Rome. Cornelia had to stay behind.

Caesar fled into the wild hill country in central Italy, and became a fugitive. He slept in forlorn caves, changing his hiding place from night to night. Then he became ill of fever, and almost died. Sulla's soldiers tracked him down, and were going to kill him at once. But Caesar cleverly talked his way out of this predicament. He was shaking and throbbing with fever, but had the presence of mind to offer a big bribe to the ignorant soldiers, with a promise of more money if they would bring him back to Rome.

So, again, he was brought face to face with Sulla. Again his life was in mortal danger. But this time several influential politicians and members of his family interceded for him with Sulla, and, wonder of wonders, the entire troupe of Vestal Virgins arrived in the Forum to plead that his life be saved. Even Sulla had

to pay respectful attention to the Vestal Virgins, and in the end he pardoned Caesar.

We can see from this story that Caesar, even when he was a very young man, had a knack for winning people to his side. Also, the impact of his personality was such that all sorts of people were willing to stand up for him, no matter what the risk.

In fact, Sulla himself was much impressed by Caesar. "Very well, I won't kill him," Sulla said. "But look out for this young man. There are several Mariuses in him."

Now that he had his pardon, Caesar thought that it would be prudent to get out of Italy for a while. So he set sail for Asia and the East. He was only twenty-one years old, and the world shone radiantly before him.

✾ V ✾

Out in the East

Out in the East, young Caesar occupied himself with several matters. Because of his family connections and also because he was enterprising, he received a good appointment almost at once and became aide-de-camp to the Roman governor of Asia Province. This was what we call Asia Minor nowadays, and more or less corresponds to contemporary Turkey. Caesar spent about three years in this province and its nearby territories, from 81 to 78 B.C.

Asia was full of commotion then. It was the eastern Roman frontier, and in some respects it resembled the Wild West of American frontier days. The Romans were spreading out into the countryside, penetrating unknown areas and subduing the inhabitants, much as the Americans fought and subdued the Indian tribes.

But the inhabitants of Asia in those days were not all savages, by any means. They derived from a long-established civilization, and in some respects were more sophisticated than the brawny Romans. One Asian king was Mithridates, who ruled a country called Pontus on the far shores of the Black Sea. He was an extraordinary man. Legend has it that he spoke twenty-two languages, had a great reputation as an art collector, practiced magic with brilliant success, and was guilty of the murder of his own mother, sister, wife, and sons. Rome had to fight three stubborn wars before Mithridates was finally subdued.

Now for the first time Caesar, full of zest and confidence, found himself in battle. He had never known combat before. The Romans were besieging a town named Mytilene, and Caesar advanced with his troops under a hail of arrows. One of his companions fell, gravely wounded, and Caesar, at the risk of his own life, dragged him to safety. This was Caesar's baptism of fire, and he acquitted himself with honor. In fact, he was awarded a high decoration, the Oak Leaf Crown.

The governor then sent Caesar as an emissary to the court of a nearby kingdom, Bithynia. He wanted to see what kind of diplomat Caesar would make. The king of Bithynia, Nicomedes, was an extrava-

gant character. He was not as important a king as
Mithridates, but still important enough. The Romans wanted him to help them raise a fleet for their
next military operations along the Asia Minor shore,
near the site of Troy and the Dardanelles. Caesar
was warmly welcomed by the young King Nicomedes. They found that they had tastes in common,
and became fast friends. So Caesar accomplished
his first diplomatic mission with distinct success.

Word now came from Rome that Sulla, exhausted
by debauchery, had died. This cleared the field for
Caesar at home, and he returned to Rome as soon
as possible. There would certainly be a struggle for
power after Sulla's death, and he wanted to be part
of what went on.

Caesar decided to plunge into politics. He sought
about for the best way to do this, and took advantage of a big scandal that was agitating Rome.
Several Roman governors had been looting their overseas provinces, and the citizenry was aroused. Cleverly, Caesar attempted to gain from this situation,
so that he would become popular with the public.
He brought an action in the law courts against a
former consul named Dolabella. Every citizen had
the right to bring a legal action of this kind, but it
was unusual for a man as youthful and inexperienced as Caesar to do so. He was pitting himself

against a prominent citizen who had full Senatorial support.

Caesar said that Dolabella, during his term as governor of Macedonia, had been flagrantly corrupt, and demanded an accounting. Caesar lost the case, but it was a gallant failure. Then he brought a similar case against another former governor who was guilty of even more looting than Dolabella. He lost this case too. The Senate Optimates were too strong for him. But both these cases helped Caesar make a name for himself as a courageous young man.

Caesar decided to return to the East. (It was on this trip that he had his adventure with the pirates.) He lived in Rhodes for a time, studying with Apollonius Molo, and resumed his friendship with King Nicomedes. Then the King of Pontus, Mithridates, broke loose and attacked the Romans in another bloody war. Caesar at once joined up and flung himself into the fighting.

This time, instead of being on the governor's staff, he became a kind of freebooter. He raised his own corps of volunteer troops, which acted as a semi-independent force.

Actually, Caesar was merely marking time out in Asia. The center of his thought was always Rome. Rome was everything. Now a new kind of opportunity came to him.

Caesar had an uncle named Cotta. For many years Cotta had been a member of the College of Pontiffs, a kind of religious tribunal which also carried political prestige and power. Cotta died suddenly, and his place in the College of Pontiffs thus became vacant.

Aurelia, Caesar's mother, got in touch with Caesar at once and urged him to return to Rome and make a bid for Cotta's post. This Caesar did, and he got it. So now his real career in Rome began.

❧ VI ❧

How Rome Was Ruled—the Senate
and the People

Caesar worked dutifully at his job as a member of the College of Pontiffs, and at the same time never ceased looking ahead. What should be his next move? What was the best possible way to advance further? He was determined to reach the top.

After taking stock of the situation he decided that it would be best to proceed in a strictly constitutional manner, and go up the regular ladder step by step. Rome was sick of violence, and the horrors of the Sulla regime hung heavily on the people.

To climb swiftly and effectively Caesar knew that he needed three things. First, a solid position with the people. Second, money. Third, military experience and force. He set about systematically to gain all three.

Meantime it was a pleasure to relax with his fam-

ily. He saw his mother, Aurelia, constantly, as well
as Julia, Marius' widow and his aunt. And, although he enjoyed friendships with other women,
he became increasingly devoted to Cornelia, his
wife, and adored their infant daughter, Julia.

Politically, when Caesar looked to the right, he
saw the Senate. There were 600 senators now. Sulla,
to strengthen his own power, had doubled the number from 300. All held their posts for life. Important magistrates, on reaching a certain political level,
became senators automatically.

When Caesar looked to the left he saw the people, the plebeian citizens of Rome. They were organized into various popular assemblies which had
substantial power.

But even though there were deep divisions in
Roman society, the people believed in unity. They
thought of themselves as being Roman *citizens,* no
matter what their rank. The entire community felt
itself bound together into a single unit. The symbol of Rome was SPQR—*Senatus Populusque Romanus*—which, translated into English, means the
Senate and People of Rome.

What were the successive steps that Caesar would
have to take to ascend the political ladder? There
were four principal ranks among the executive of-

ficers who administered the Roman state, and a rising politician was required to be chosen for each in turn.

First, the *quaestors*. These were officers who tended to the budget, checked expenditures, and were responsible for finances.

Second, the *aediles*, who supervised civic affairs in general, including such matters as water supply, roads, the public games, and repair of buildings.

Third, the *praetors*, senior magistrates or judges. A praetorship was a very important post.

Finally, in supreme authority, there were the two *consuls*. These were a combination of president and prime minister, and were the chief officers of the government. If a consul was a strong man he was in a position to rule Rome. For generations only patricians were allowed to be consuls. But now, in Caesar's time, the situation had changed so much that one consul *had* to be a plebeian, and both could be.

In a different category, the *tribunes* were important. These were men specifically charged with safeguarding the people's rights in all state affairs. They were the representatives of the plebeians exclusively; their persons were sacred, and they had the power to veto any measure passed by the Senate.

Tribunes had to keep their houses open all night, so that people in trouble could get to them quickly. No patrician could be a tribune.

Seldom has any constitution had so many checks and balances as the Roman constitution. For instance the consuls, the supreme officers of state, could in theory serve for only one one-year term, and could not be elected again until ten years had passed. (This rule, however, had been broken frequently.) Moreover, there were always *two* consuls, not just one, and these had equal powers. Each consul could exercise a veto over the other. Still again, every consul—in fact every public servant in Rome—could be haled before a court at any time and made to give an account of himself right down to the end of his life. A former consul could be tried for events that had happened in his consulship years before.

Obviously, the Roman system was democracy of such a pure type (in theory) that it was always in danger of nullifying itself. Officials used the veto so much that on some occasions no laws could be passed at all. This was what made it easy for unscrupulous strong men, like Sulla, to leap into the breach and seize power for themselves.

Another important point was that the great executive posts in the Roman government were *unpaid.*

There was no salary attached to being a tribune or a praetor or a consul. (This may seem strange to us, but it is worth noting that until quite recently members of the British House of Commons were not paid for their services.) In Rome the fact that the most important jobs were unpaid meant, of course, that only rich men could afford to hold office. This naturally strengthened the hand of the patricians in the Senate, which was still full of wealthy men.

The makers of the Roman constitution realized that in circumstances of sudden crisis their system would not work well. Leadership might be paralyzed. So a loophole was provided whereby a single *dictator* might be appointed by the consuls, with the consent of the Senate. This dictator could, moreover, have an assistant known as the Master of the Horse. But the dictator could not legally hold office for more than six months.

Also the custom arose whereby a praetor or consul could, after his year's term of office, go out into the field somewhere as an administrator or governor. He was then called a *pro-praetor* or *pro-consul*. This was a development of prime importance. Ambitious men sought to become consuls not so much for the dignity this brought during the year's term of office in Rome itself, but for the opportunity it

gave them to be colonial governors later. Then, with
luck, and if they were greedy or unscrupulous, they
could loot whole provinces at will. Once a man was
a pro-consul out of Rome, he could do virtually anything he wished.

Finally—and this was what interested Caesar
most—the Roman army had become a major factor
in all public and political affairs. Both Marius and
Sulla contributed to this evolution. Marius transformed the old militia, a citizen's army made up
mostly of peasant volunteers, into an altogether new
type of professional fighting force. The celebrated
Roman legions, with their matchless discipline, har-
dihood, and fighting spirit, came out of his reforms.

In theory the army was the servant and protector
of the state. But Sulla used *his* legions to further
his own advance, and twice led his armed forces
into Rome. Thus it came about that the legions no
longer gave their first loyalty necessarily to the state,
but to their own individual commander, who fed
and paid them.

By Caesar's time, no Roman leader had any
chance of reaching supreme power unless the army
backed him, or until he had built up an army of
his own. The first law of politics was *to get a command*. But to get a command, a man had to be a
praetor or a consul first.

❦ VII ❦

The Political Arena

In 68 B.C. Caesar decided to run for quaestor. But
to run for office cost an enormous sum in those days,
and Caesar was hard up. He could not afford to
finance an election himself. Hence a very important
personage entered his story—the financier Crassus—
who was destined to be involved with him for many
years to come.

To run for office cost so much money because
Rome had become unimaginably corrupt. Roman
citizenship had been extended to most of Italy, and
this made the process of voting cumbersome and
difficult. Politicians bribed voters left and right, and
immense blocks of votes were bought and sold. In
order to win, a candidate had to be able to buy
votes wholesale, and prices rose. To run for consul
could cost a man $500,000.

Crassus was the wealthiest man in Rome, and he was not at all an admirable character. He had accumulated part of his vast fortune, which probably amounted to $50,000,000, by shady means. For instance, during Sulla's day he would contrive to find out what victims were going to be "proscribed," and then buy up their properties for a song. Crassus even operated his own private fire department, historians tell us. If a fire broke out in someone's house, he would send his fire engines there but his firemen would not put out the fire unless the householder paid Crassus handsomely.

Crassus was greedy, and continually searched for new ways to make money by graft or speculation. Also he was cruel. He held several military commands. It was he who put down a famous revolt of the slaves led by the gladiator Spartacus. He vanquished the heroic Spartacus after a grueling fight, and celebrated his victory by having six thousand slaves crucified on the Appian Way, the principal road leading into Rome.

One of his Roman legions failed him on one occasion, and he subjected it to a terrible penalty: Every tenth man, chosen by lot, was killed. Such was the man who now became Caesar's chief supporter and close friend.

Caesar won the election for the quaestorship easily, but in order to buy enough votes he had to borrow large sums from Crassus. This established a pattern which was to last for a good many years. Caesar was perpetually in debt to Crassus and other wealthy men. He had to borrow large amounts of money not merely in order to be elected to office, but also to maintain himself in office after election. This was because a politician, to be well regarded, had to spend considerable sums out of his own pocket for the entertainment of the public at festivals, gladiatorial games, and other ceremonies.

One of Caesar's chief defects was his careless attitude toward money. He was almost always heavily in debt, yet he never seemed to worry about this at all. He was certain that Crassus or some other financier would rescue him eventually, because he was, so to speak, a good investment. He was sure to get a great command some day, to become rich, and be able to pay back what he owed. Also, he was rapidly becoming an influential politician, and hence was in a position to do important favors for his creditors, which was another way of repaying them.

Yet Caesar did an exceptionally good job as quaestor. He worked hard and watched the people's interest. He was diligent and painstaking.

There were twenty quaestors at this time and the

post was not very important unless it was in the hands of an energetic man. But quaestors automatically became members of the Senate, and so Caesar, at the early age of thirty-four, reached membership in this eminent body. The situation was picturesque, because Caesar was a keen antagonist of most of the older conservative senators. The Senate now had a viper in its midst. But, as a matter of fact, Caesar never paid much attention to the Senate, and seldom attended its sessions except when this was strictly necessary. He was more interested in other avenues to power.

As quaestor, he spent money like water. His debts soon amounted to 830 talents, or $830,000. But Crassus was there to bail him out.

One thing that has puzzled historians for two thousand years is what Caesar really thought of the people, whom he was pledged to serve. He was a people's man, but later he became a dictator *over* the people. What did he care for most—his own advancement or the good of the people as a whole? Did he merely *use* the people to serve his own ends? The fairest answer seems to be that, although he was ambitious in the extreme, he always felt himself deeply rooted in the people and, as a rule, pursued policies that he genuinely thought would benefit the people and make Rome a stronger, stabler, happier state.

During his quaestorship Caesar suffered a severe double personal loss. His aunt Julia died, and so did his youthful wife, Cornelia. Caesar calmly took political advantage of both these tragedies. He gave Julia a magnificent public funeral, and in his oration emphasized the fact that the Julian family, of which he was now the head, could claim both divine and royal blood. Also he was bold enough to mention Marius and even to exhibit a bust of Marius prominently in Julia's funeral procession. Ever since Sulla it had been absolutely forbidden to talk about Marius in public, or to honor him. Caesar brought him out into the open again. This greatly impressed the crowds at large and members of the Populare party, and Caesar's reputation grew as a man devoted to the people's interest.

Also he insisted on giving Cornelia a large and impressive funeral, and made a speech in the Forum about her. This was an unusual thing to do, since there was nothing in Cornelia's position to justify such an honor. But the public, always eager for something new and colorful, liked Caesar for his unconventionality and enterprise.

Caesar had been fond of Cornelia. Their marriage

had been happy, although he had been a difficult husband at times and was often away from Rome. But his happiness with Cornelia did not keep him from marrying another lady almost at once—Pompeia. She was an altogether different type from Cornelia. Cornelia had been the typical young Roman matron, correct and dutiful. But Pompeia was something of an adventuress, beautiful, light-minded, and fond of pleasure. Nor was that all. She was *Sulla's* granddaughter! Caesar was now marrying into the family of his hated enemy, the despot Sulla!

However, it is doubtful if politics had much to do with Caesar's new marriage. He did not gain much, from the point of view of his career, by being con-

nected with the Sulla group. What the match really indicated was that Rome was a town where almost everybody was related to everybody else, and where, then as now, strictly personal considerations often cut across family, political, or social bonds.

❦ VIII ❦

Caesar Struggles to Get Ahead

Next, Caesar got an administrative post in Spain, which had been a Roman province for some time. He journeyed to Spain by way of northern Italy (Cisalpine Gaul) and southern France. He spent one night in a miserably forlorn, dirty little village, and one of his lieutenants asked him grimly, "How would you like to live in this awful place?" Caesar replied, "I would rather be first man here than second man in Rome."

Spain taught Caesar a great deal. He was as fascinated by the ways of life of this strange country as he had been by the East, and he learned at firsthand about difficult colonial problems and how to deal with them.

In the town of Cadiz Caesar came across a statue of Alexander the Great, stared at it for a long moment, and then burst out weeping. His comrades, shocked, asked him why he was giving way to emotion in such an un-Roman way.

Caesar replied, "Don't you think I have good cause to weep? Alexander was no older when he died than I am now, and think of all that he accomplished. But I have done nothing!"

Returning to Rome, Caesar spent some time in Cisalpine Gaul, and found that this province was boiling with unrest. The Italians here did not have Roman citizenship as yet, and wanted it badly. It occurred to Caesar that he might further his own interests dramatically by inciting the Cisalpine Gauls to revolt against Roman authority. According to one old historian, he even dabbled with the idea of plotting to kill off a group of conservative senators. But he decided in the end not to foment any revolution or otherwise make trouble. The time was not yet ripe.

The lesson of this episode is that, although he wanted to advance himself by constitutional means, ambition was egging him on to the use of desperate measures. Also it shows the general moral anarchy of the time, which influenced even the highest minds. Intrigue dominated everything in Rome, and Caesar, if only to keep up with his rivals, had to think in terms of conspiracy and possible violence.

Caesar took his next big step upward by being elected aedile when he was about thirty-seven years old. The election cost him even more than the previous one for the quaestorship, and in addition he spent fantastic sums during his term. It was part of the job of the aediles to amuse the populace, and Caesar outdid anybody in the history of Rome by his extravagance. For just one performance in the arena he hired no fewer than 640 gladiators, and had them armored in silver. His debts increased enormously, but he never even bothered to keep accounts.

Soon he had so many private gladiators that the Senate thought he was building up a private army. To keep him in check, the Senate passed a law restricting the number of combatants that could appear at festivals and games.

But all of this made Caesar even more popular with the mob, the man on the street, and he became leader of the Populare party. To confirm his position, he defied convention once more by giving a large public display in honor of Marius. Also, at his own expense, he rebuilt and decorated the Appian Way.

He also entertained lavishly at home, and widened his circle of acquaintances. One event of this year was that he contrived to marry off one of his sisters, Julia, to a rich profiteer and moneylender.

Then Caesar became Pontifex Maximus. This was not a post in the regular order of succession, and he had no real right to it. Nobody so young had ever been Pontifex Maximus before. Nor did he have the proper spiritual qualifications. The Pontifex Maximus was, after all, the head of the principal college of priests. But when the post suddenly became vacant, Caesar determined to make a try for it, and managed to get it by clever politics and bribery.

Whether he would actually be confirmed as Pontifex Maximus was uncertain for a while. Caesar was taking grave risks. He told his mother, "I'll be Pontifex Maximus by tonight or I'll be exiled from Rome."

He was not exiled from Rome. His position as Pontifex Maximus was not only confirmed but became an important aid to his career. It served to make him respected in the eyes of the conservatives, and he was now entitled to live in an official residence.

By this time, as was natural, Caesar had made several bitter enemies. They were not only jealous, but detested him on general principles. One enemy was Cato the Younger. Cato was a severe, disciplined young moralist. He was the great-grandson of the formidable Cato who had told the Romans, during the Punic wars a hundred years before, that their enemy Carthage must be utterly destroyed. He was a man of medium height, lean, with a broad high forehead and a craggy nose.

Another enemy—at times—was the renowned orator, Cicero, whom Caesar had known since childhood. Cicero was an active politician as well as a literary man. He played hot and cold with Caesar. Sometimes he opposed him, sometimes not.

Caesar also had some interesting friends and henchmen. One was Titus Labienus, who did most of the underground work in arranging for Caesar to become Pontifex Maximus, and who was later to become Caesar's best general. Another was a man of totally different caliber, Clodius. The youthful Clodius was a wild scamp, but he was useful because he was devoted to Caesar and led gangs of young men on the streets who became part of Caesar's "mob."

Caesar got into trouble on occasion. People thought that he was going too far. He was even accused of plotting to set himself up as a tyrant in Egypt. But he played his cards well, and wriggled out of various difficulties. He was one of the greatest pullers of strings who ever lived, and his basic strength came from the fact that all the poor and needy, as an eminent historian says, "put their hopes

in him." He was both party boss and civic leader. He promised bread, land, and citizenship.

The year 63 B.C. was an agitated one. Cicero was consul. Then came the celebrated Catiline conspiracy. Catiline was a young nobleman who aspired greatly to power. He promised to cancel the people's debts and to divide up the great estates and give them to the needy. There is no doubt that both Crassus and Caesar, to an extent, were involved with Catiline. But news of his conspiracy to seize the government leaked out, he was forced to flee, and his chief associates were arrested. Later Catiline himself was killed in battle. Cicero, after a series of furious orations which students still read, had the other conspirators condemned to death and executed. Caesar, at great risk, did his best to save them and

have their sentences commuted to life imprison-
ment, but failed. Cicero, at this moment, was too
strong for him.

One colorful episode connected with the conspiracy has come down to us. One of Caesar's closest
friends was a lady named Servilia. She was a half-
sister of his enemy Cato, and also was the mother of
Marcus Brutus, who was to be the chief of Caesar's
assassins some years later. During a violent debate
in the Senate a messenger brought Caesar a private
letter. Cato demanded to see it, thinking that it
might be a document incriminating Caesar with Catiline. Caesar glanced at the letter quickly and then,
without a word, passed it calmly to the angry Cato.
Cato then saw that it was a love letter from Servilia
to Caesar. Cato's rage knew no bounds. He threw
the letter in Caesar's face, yelling, "Take it back,
you drunkard!" Now Caesar, for all his faults, was
not a drunkard and everybody knew that he was not,
and so Cato was made to seem ridiculous.

Finally, at about this time, Caesar was elected
praetor. He was forty years old and had almost, but
not quite, reached the top.

❀ IX ❀

Pompey, Crassus, and the Triumvirate

One crisis during Caesar's praetorship was of domestic origin. It had to do with Pompeia, his wife, and the rascal Clodius, his close friend.

Once a year Roman society matrons, the ladies of good family, celebrated an occasion known as the Feast of the Good Goddess under the supervision of the Vestal Virgins. Secret rites, which were sacred in the extreme, took place at this feast, from which all men were rigorously excluded. It came Pompeia's turn to give the annual feast of the Good Goddess in Caesar's house. Caesar, as was the custom, left the house for the day. The women proceeded with their occult ceremonies. Then it was discovered that Clodius, disguised as a singing girl, had managed to make his way secretly into the house, and had watched all that went on and had even taken part in the festivities.

Aurelia, Caesar's mother, sent Caesar a message asking him to return home immediately. Caesar did so. Clodius was found hiding in the room of Pompeia's maid. The scandal was terrific. The crime of profaning the holy rites was so serious that Clodius was charged with high treason. He stood trial, but managed to avoid punishment.

A few days later, Caesar divorced Pompeia. There was no proof that she had done anything wrong, but Caesar felt that he had to get rid of her because of the scandal. Possibly he was tired of her by this time, but in any case he did not want any taint of unpleasantness to be attached to his household, even if she were innocent. He proclaimed to everybody, "Caesar's wife must be above suspicion!"

Caesar did not, however, break off relations with Clodius. He could not help being fond of this young man. Besides, Clodius and his gang of toughs were increasingly useful.

In fact Caesar needed Clodius' help so badly that he decided to make him a tribune. But Clodius was a patrician, and tribunes had to be plebeians. So Caesar contrived to have Clodius *adopted* into a plebeian family, so that he could call himself a plebeian and be elected to the tribuneship. Citizens perked up their ears at this, especially since Clodius was a year or two older than his new "father"! But

Caesar succeeded in this outlandish maneuver, and Clodius served him well. As for Pompeia, she was forgotten.

As praetor Caesar distinguished himself chiefly by being a fair-minded and able judge. Also he worked hard at other tasks, and learned about the administrative problems of a great city.

After his praetorship, and when he was forty-one years old, Caesar got the governorship of Spain. This was his first important command. He was now, for the first time in his career, head of an army, because the governor of a province always had an army at his disposal. Had Caesar not succeeded in getting this command, he would have been ruined, and he knew it. His debts now amounted to $3,250,000, the biggest in the history of Rome, and his creditors tried to attach all his property and keep him from going to Spain.

Then, once more, Crassus and other rich men bailed him out. In Spain he collected immense sums, as every governor did, by taking a share of the local taxes and selling prisoners of war into slavery. This was considered to be a perfectly proper and correct thing to do. In a year Caesar became wealthy enough to pay off all his debts, and was never seriously in debt again. Money problems were now behind him.

Caesar did a first-rate job in Spain. He fought
a small war, subdued an army of rebels in a district
called Lusitania, reached Galicia (a territory hither-
to unconquered) and looked on the Atlantic Ocean
for the first time. More than this, he proved himself
to be an excellent administrator. He worked out
financial and other reforms, and set up an efficient,
just regime.

But all the time he was thinking of Rome more
than anything else. He had determined to stand for
the consulship, the supreme prize, the next year.

Now at this point we must have a word about
the great Roman soldier and commander, Pompey.
The lives of Caesar and Pompey became intertwined
at about this time, and it is impossible to write about
Caesar without writing about Pompey too.

Pompey was far and away the most important man
in Rome. Caesar was coming forward swiftly, but he
was still a midget compared to the giant Pompey.
Pompey had had a magnificent career. He was born
in 106 B.C., and was thus four years older than
Caesar. He began military life as a protégé of Sulla's.
He fought well in the civil wars, and helped to conquer Spain. In fact his accomplishments were so
brilliant that he was given the name "Magnus,"
meaning "Great," while he was still in his early
thirties.

Rome depended for its food supply on overseas shipping. But swarms of pirates infested the Mediterranean, gravely interfering with the import of food, and even attacked the shores of Italy itself. The Senate gave Pompey an extraordinary three years' command over the whole Mediterranean, in order to subdue the pirates. Pompey got rid of the pirates in eighty days, sweeping them from the seas. The Mediterranean became safe, and Rome never had to worry about its food supply again.

Then Pompey went on to Asia. Here too his victories were extraordinary. He won several wars and, among other things, was active in straightening out affairs in Jerusalem. He fought no fewer than 107 battles, and founded no fewer than thirty cities. He planted these cities everywhere in the East to open the way to Roman colonization. Then he reorganized all of Roman Asia into four giant provinces.

Twice, returning to Rome after his victorious campaigns, the glittering Pompey had been honored with what was known as a "triumph," the huge celebration with which Rome greeted a conqueror. A triumph, with its attendant ceremonies, was the biggest single thing that could happen in a citizen's life, and was full of gladiators, chariot races, purple robes, feasts, captured enemies, lions, and elephants. No one had ever been given two triumphs before.

As for politics, Pompey started out as a conservative Optimate, became a Populare, and then switched to being an Optimate again.

Pompey was a heavily built man, with the bull neck characteristic of Romans, but very good-looking. He was called the handsomest man in Rome. Moreover, his personality was pleasing. His chief defect was an overpowering vanity. Also he was a bad politician, and in the end this proved to be his ruin. Like many gifted military men, he was not particularly bright about things outside his own military realm.

Caesar knew well that, to get further in his own career, he would have to make terms with Pompey. Yet he was still insignificant compared to Pompey. There was one thing, however, that helped Caesar considerably when his negotiations with Pompey began: While Pompey was away in Asia, Caesar had become a good friend of Mucia, Pompey's wife.

Back in Rome after his period of office in Spain, Caesar set out to run for the consulship.

He had several irritating setbacks. For one thing the Senate, controlled by the Optimates, refused to let him have a triumph in spite of his victories in Spain. His opponents said that he had provoked an unnecessary war there in order to gain fame and riches. For another, the Senate decided that the consuls for the next year should *not,* on completion

of their terms, get any big lucrative posts abroad.

Caesar was always looking ahead and, like most great men, lived more in the future than the present. The chief reason he wanted to be consul was, of course, to get the really big command that usually followed a consulship when the consul became a pro-consul out of Rome.

But the Senate decided that Caesar, on completing his year as consul, should get nothing but an appointment that was so minor as to be insulting—commissioner of forests!

Caesar's brilliant countermove was to create what history calls the First Triumvirate. This consisted of Caesar, Crassus, and Pompey, and it ruled Rome for the next few years. Working together, these three men were invincible. Pompey had the army, Crassus had the money, and Caesar, a political genius, had the support of the people. The Triumvirate was formed in 60 B.C., and Caesar was duly elected to the consulship the next year.

But why should Crassus and Pompey have wanted to join Caesar in this Triumvirate? What did they gain from it?

There were several reasons. As far as Crassus was concerned, he and Pompey were bitterly jealous of each other. The partnership was an insurance that Pompey would not move to destroy Crassus. Also,

Crassus was promised rich tax collections in Asia. Even so, for Caesar to have brought these two rivals together was a major feat. It took every bit of artfulness, political skill and strength he possessed.

As for Pompey, he joined the Triumvirate because he badly needed political support. He wanted two things above all: first, land for his troops which had returned to Italy; second, ratification by the government of the new territorial arrangements he had made in Asia. And Caesar, as consul, would be by far the best man to help him get both these things.

Of course, it was Caesar himself who gained most from the Triumvirate. Not only was he consul, but he was firmly associated with the two most powerful men in Rome. Both Pompey and Crassus were now on his side.

Then came some startling personal arrangements. Pompey obtained a divorce from Mucia, his wife. And Julia, the young daughter of Caesar, married Pompey. This sensational event naturally served to seal the alliance between Caesar and Pompey, and Caesar was highly pleased. Pompey, although four years Caesar's senior, was now his son-in-law! Of course he was many years older than Julia, his new bride. Yet the marriage was a genuine love match, and a very happy one.

Then Caesar also decided to marry again. The bride he chose, his fourth, was named Calpurnia. She was a good and loyal woman, he was extremely fond of her, and she remained his wife until his death. The marriage had political overtones, since Calpurnia was the daughter of a prominent politician, Piso. And as Caesar never missed an opportunity to use private relationships for political gain, he arranged for Piso to become consul the next year. Piso, as consul, would be a useful ally.

Caesar's puritanical enemy Cato, blind with fury and outraged by these developments, rose in the Senate to denounce Caesar. He called the gods to witness that it was "a shameful matter, not to be suffered," that politicians should "make havoc of the empire of Rome with horrible bawdy matches," and distribute provinces and armies to themselves through "wicked marriages."

Caesar paid no attention to this criticism and proceeded to do an excellent job as consul. He set up a system whereby the proceedings of the Senate were recorded every day, as in our *Congressional Record;* this had never been done before, and was an important reform. He managed—temporarily—to get rid of both his chief enemies, Cicero and Cato, by packing them off overseas. He gave great amounts of land to the needy, took care of the veterans, and

passed strict laws to prevent corruption by provin-
cial governors. He dominated proceedings so much
that the other consul, a conservative named Bibulus,
never had anything to say, and wits called the con-
sulate that of "Julius *and* Caesar," with Bibulus left
out.

Meantime, with the help of his two partners in
the Triumvirate, Crassus and Pompey, he succeeded
in nullifying the Senate decision which had given
him the lowly post of commissioner of forests for
the next year. He never stopped maneuvering to get
a really great command. Finally, by using every wile
and device, he was assigned the pro-consulship for
Cisalpine Gaul and Illyria, the frontier region on the
other side of the Adriatic which today is called Dal-
matia. Moreover, he succeeded in getting the command over these territories not merely for the usual
term of one year, but for five years.

On top of this came a stroke of unexpected, overwhelming luck. The man who had Transalpine Gaul
—the Gaul beyond the Alps, which was much more
important that Cisalpine Gaul—died suddenly, and
Caesar was given this enormous command as well.

So, at the age of forty-four, Caesar set out for
Gaul, and his great years, his tremendous years,
began.

PART II

❧ X ❧

Caesar Conquers Gaul

It was 58 B.C. when Caesar started his Gallic campaigns. Gaul was very rich in natural resources, particularly minerals. To gain these was one reason why Rome wanted to conquer Gaul. But a more important motive was fear of invasion by Gaul's fierce, aggressive people.

His enemies in Rome scoffed when Caesar started out for Gaul. They laughed. They thought they were getting rid of him by sending him out to waste himself in the wilderness.

Caesar knew that Cisalpine Gaul, one division of his command, provided an ideal strategic position; he could look both north and south. He was close enough to the north to know what was going on up there, and near enough to Rome to keep in close touch with politics. Usually Caesar spent his winters in the valley of the Po, and sometimes he went as far south as the town of Ravenna, which was only about two hundred miles from Rome. Of course he could not return to Rome itself as long as he held an active military command. It was an absolutely fixed Roman rule that no military man could enter the sacred precincts of the city until he had disbanded his troops.

At this point we should have a word about Gaul itself. Not all of Gaul was savage. Cisalpine Gaul, the part below the Alps, had been under Roman dominion for many years. Also Rome held a narrow strip of Gaul along the Mediterranean which was named "The Province." (This corresponds today to the French Riviera and what we still call "Provence." The Romans conquered it early because it was their main pathway to Spain.)

Moreover, several Gallic chieftains in the far interior had sworn allegiance to Rome, or had become Roman puppets. Many Gauls served willingly in the Roman army, and some tribes were faithful Roman allies.

The Gauls were barbarians by Roman standards, but they had many good qualities. They were big men physically, splendid fighters and expert horsemen. They were tough, durable, and full of courage. Caesar admired their military traits.

They had roads of a kind, cities of a kind, good weapons, and a rude form of currency. Their primitive social organization was dominated by a fierce semi-priesthood class, the Druids. Few knew how to read or write.

Most Gauls lived in what is France and Belgium today, and were a Celtic people. To the east were other primitive tribesmen who were often hostile, such as the Helvetii (Swiss) and Germans. Often the Germans made big raids into Celtic territory, and sought to push the Gauls back and take their land.

We should also have a word about the Roman army in Caesar's time. Six hundred men made a cohort, and ten cohorts made a legion. The average strength of a legion was, in other words, six thousand men. These were professional troops, highly trained infantrymen. They were armed with a helmet, a shield, a long javelin, and a short, broad, keen-edged sword.

Caesar's army consisted of only three legions when he got the command in Gaul, and he recruited one more in Cisalpine Gaul before the campaign began. He never had more than ten or eleven legions in all. He was the first Roman commander to number his legions and to give each its own identity.

Caesar's favorite legion was the Tenth. It was a

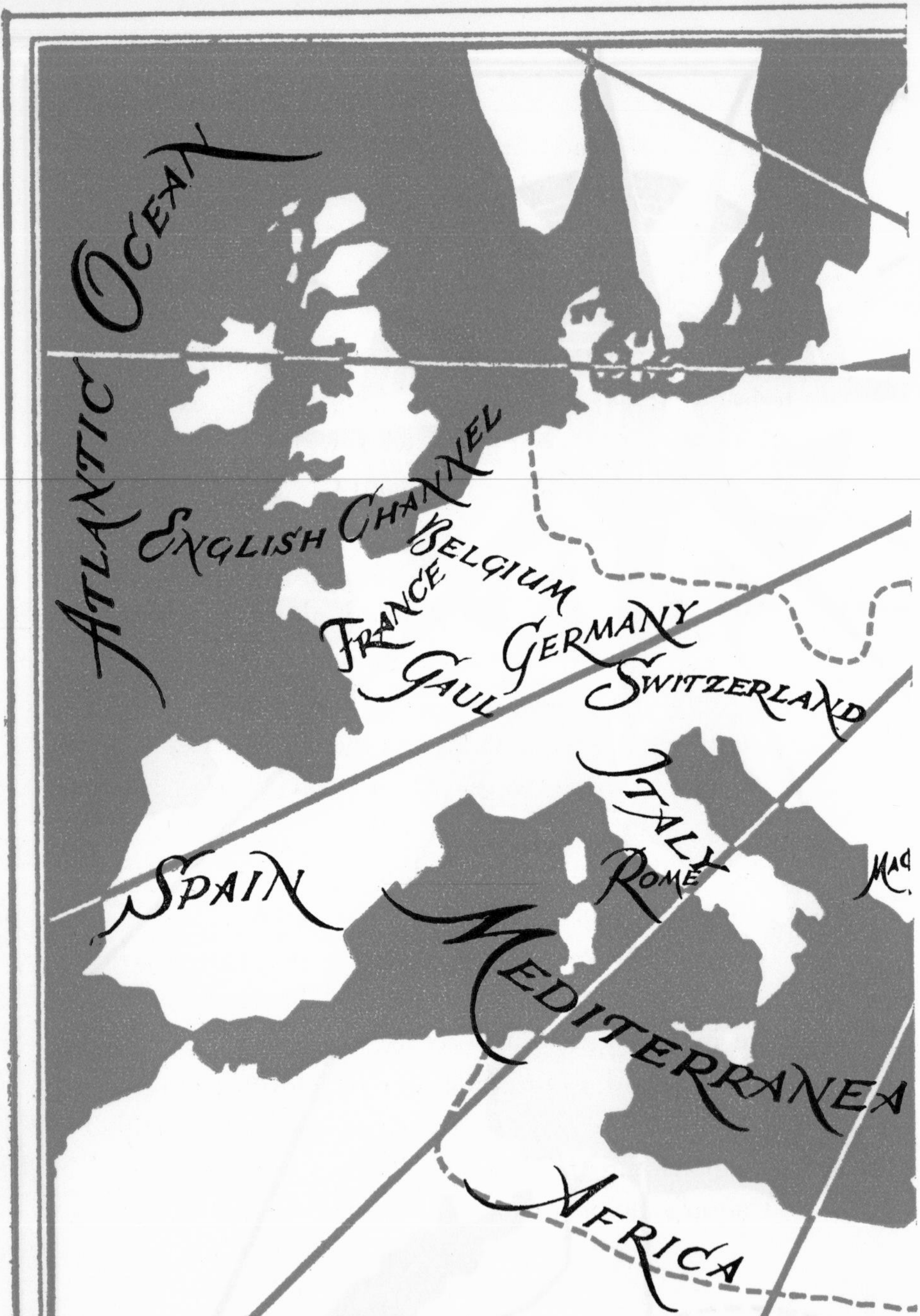
ATLANTIC OCEAN
ENGLISH CHANNEL
BELGIUM
FRANCE
GAUL
GERMANY
SWITZERLAND
ITALY
ROME
SPAIN
MEDITERRANEA
AFRICA

first-class legion indeed. Sometimes Caesar personally carried its "Eagle" (standard) into battle.

While campaigning, Caesar's forces marched many miles a day. They were extremely well disciplined. Every time they stopped for the night, no matter how exhausted they might be, they built a solid fortified camp—almost a small walled town—in order to be able to resist any surprise attack.

Legionnaires under Caesar were not merely combat troops but also expert engineers. They carried tools as well as arms, and had to be able to build bridges, lay down roads through swamps, construct complex fortifications, and operate huge siege-trains.

The cavalry was a force apart, and usually consisted of auxiliaries. Caesar often recruited his cavalry from friendly Gauls or even from Gauls whom he had vanquished. Sometimes, in an emergency, he simply put a Roman infantryman on a horse, and presto! the infantryman was a cavalryman from that time on.

Caesar and his staff did their work through men known as centurions. These were like our master sergeants of today, but had more authority. There were sixty centurions to a legion.

Also, each legion had several officials known as "military tribunes." These were usually appointed by the supreme commander to serve his special ends, and their duties were often more political than military.

Caesar was a wonderfully good tactician. His standard plan for battle was to draw his legions, divided into cohorts, into three broad, firm lines. The first line led the attack, and the others were reserves which could move swiftly to either side. Caesar made the Roman army much more supple and flexible than it had been before. He did not rely so much on numbers as on quick, unexpected movement. But he always saved a solid block of infantrymen to make the final assault, and his sense of timing was acute.

Above all, a Roman legion was a *personal* army. It owed its supreme duty not to the state, but to its own commander.

Caesar himself is the best source of information for the great Gallic campaigns. His book, *The Conquest of Gaul,* not only survives today, but is still required reading for every Latin student. Caesar wrote it partly as a record, dictating it to his secretaries every day, and partly as a document to impress Roman citizens and the Senate. Like a famous American autobiography centuries later, *The Education of Henry Adams,* it is written in the third person; only rarely does Caesar permit himself the luxury of an "I." The manuscript of Caesar's book was almost lost once when a boat overturned. Caesar swam to shore holding the precious pages aloft, and thus saved it.

Caesar's tone is always objective, and although he may give himself the benefit of the doubt sometimes and is proud of his successes, the basic accuracy of his account has never been contested. Of course he justifies practically all of his campaigns as "defensive measures." Generals always do.

Swift as a panther, Caesar set out for Gaul. He got from Rome to the Rhone River in eight days —good time for those days! It was as if he had been unleashed; as if all his life had been a preparation for this moment. Also, he moved to take up his command quickly because some of his enemies in Rome had threatened to put him on trial for various alleged illegal acts.

First Caesar had to deal with the Helvetii, or Swiss. These stout people had exhausted the soil in their mountain villages, and were setting out to migrate into Celtic territory. Caesar felt that he had to prevent this movement at all costs, because it would undermine Roman authority and weaken the Gallic tribes which were friendly to Rome.

Only one Roman legion was stationed north of the Alps at this time. So Caesar had only 6,000 men against 350,000 or more. He darted to Geneva and destroyed the bridge over the Rhone there, in order to slow up the Swiss. Then he hurried back to his headquarters in Cisalpine Gaul, picked up his other legions, and crossed the Alps with them. This was a tremendous feat, because the Alpine passes were choked with ice and snow.

By this time the Swiss had managed to reach

central France, near what is Lyons today. Caesar
met them in a great battle, and destroyed their
hosts. The surviving Helvetti were forced to return
to their homes in Switzerland.

Next, Caesar fought the Germans. One important
German chieftain was the tall, blond Ariovistus.
Until this time he had been on his good behavior,
and had not made trouble for Rome. But now he
moved threateningly against a Gallic tribe which
was a Roman ally. Caesar hunted Ariovistus down,
defeated him in a hotly contested battle in Alsace,
and forced him back to the Rhine.

Some of Caesar's troops did not yet fully realize
the mettle of their commander. They were terrified
at the idea of fighting the stalwart, dangerous
Germans. Caesar shamed them into following him
by saying that, if they stood back, he would advance
with the Tenth Legion alone. So they followed him.

Next, in 57 B.C., Caesar decided to go ahead and
subjugate all of Gaul. He did not think that the
opposition would be strong. But when he calmly
annexed two large blocks of territory, the Gauls in
other parts of Gaul decided to fight for their surviving homelands. First the Belgae (Belgians)
sought to impede Caesar's conquest. By clever strategy, Caesar forced them back without much fighting. Then a tribe to the northeast, the ferocious

Nervii, rose. Caesar beat them down in a terrific battle. Of 60,000 Nervii, only 500 escaped. Caesar led the final charge himself.

Then the savage Aduatuci rose in southern Belgium. Caesar conquered them in a swift campaign, and, because he thought that their uprising had been prompted by treachery, he sold the whole tribe into slavery.

By the year 56 B.C. most of Gaul seemed pacified. But now a strong people known as the Veneti, whose homeland was Brittany, broke loose. This was the hardest campaign Caesar had had to fight up to that time. The inhabitants of Brittany, then as now, were marvelous seamen, and they took refuge on islands which could only be reached by ships. They blockaded the coast and made forays down the rivers. The Romans had never been very skillful mariners, and Caesar was perplexed. Finally he built a fleet himself, on the river Loire, and sailed this into Brittany down other rivers. The Romans won the naval battle that followed by making use of a new weapon—long poles with sickles attached, with which they cut down the rigging of the enemy ships. So at last the rebellious Veneti were subdued.

Practically all of Gaul was now in Roman hands. Caesar thought that he had won the war. It was just as well that he was relieved of campaigning for the moment, because a severe political crisis had built up behind him in Italy. Hastily, he returned to his headquarters near the Po.

❀ XI ❀

He Has Interests in Rome, Too, While Fighting a Thousand Miles Away

The Pompey-Crassus-Caesar coalition, or Triumvirate, seemed to be in danger of breaking up. Pompey was getting restless, and Crassus felt ignored. Caesar, naturally, did not want the Triumvirate to collapse, because if it did his future position in Rome would be threatened.

He had two things to do: first, continue to win battles in Gaul, and, second, contrive to be on top in Rome when he returned. There were plenty of difficulties for him in Rome. A movement even began to deprive Caesar of his command and, in spite of his victories, to bring him back to Rome in disgrace.

Caesar's reply was to invite Pompey and Crassus to what we would call nowadays a "summit" meeting at Lucca. This town was in the southern part of Caesar's Cisalpine command, but was not too hard for Pompey, Crassus, and their retainers to reach.

The Lucca conference, which took place in 56 B.C., was a big affair. Hundreds of senators and other politicians came up from Rome to be on hand.

It was at Lucca that Mark Antony, one of the foremost Roman heroes, first entered the Caesar story. He was a bold young adventurer of good family whom Caesar had known for years but whom he had never made much use of before. Now Mark Antony became one of Caesar's most trusted agents. He was a reckless, boisterous personality, but very brave and devotedly loyal to Caesar's interests.

When Caesar got Pompey and Crassus in a room together he had the whip hand because it was he who was winning the battles. Also, Caesar was a skilled negotiator at a conference table. He played up to Pompey, who was extremely vain. And, once the three top leaders reached agreement, everybody else had to follow. Caesar "won" the Lucca conference easily.

Pompey and Crassus got a good deal out of it, however. They were to be made consuls for the next year, and after that, pro-consuls. Pompey was to get Spain and Crassus was to get a tremendous command, Syria. Meantime, Pompey would be undisputed boss in Rome. Moreover it was decided that he could run Spain by means of deputies, while remaining in Rome himself. This gave him a substantial political advantage.

But Caesar got what he wanted too. His command in Gaul, which was to expire at the end of 54 B.C., was extended for five full years. Then it was understood that he would return to Rome and stand for consul in 48 B.C., which meant that he would be running Rome too after that date.

So, with his future in Gaul secured and his fences seemingly mended at home, Caesar returned swiftly to the front. He faced a sudden dangerous situation.

Two German tribes were penetrating northward into what we call Flanders today. Now Caesar did something for which he has been blamed ever since. The old adage is that all is fair in love and war, but Caesar seems to have gone a long way in overstepping the bounds of correct behavior.

He called a parley with the German leaders. They accepted, and came peaceably to his camp. Then, although they were protected under the flag of truce, he arrested them on the charge, probably trumped up, that their followers behind the lines

had violated the armistice agreement. He ordered
them to be executed, and then took advantage of
this to massacre their troops to a man. More than
400,000 Germans died.

This course of action by Caesar provoked vehe-
ment indignation in Rome. The old Rome, with its
high ethical standards, had not yet quite dis-
appeared. The stern Cato, for one, who was now
back in Rome, accused Caesar of treacherous conduct, and demanded that he be brought back home
to be punished, or handed over to the Germans to
be dealt with as they liked.

Caesar paid little attention to Cato's accusations.
He had an important objective in view. He wanted
to get into Germany, and he was determined to
cross the Rhine. It had never been bridged before,
but his men built a bridge across this broad, foam-
ing river in the incredible time of ten days. Then
Caesar crossed the Rhine, not far from where the
Americans crossed it in 1945, and boldly thrust
his way into Germany. It was the first time Roman
forces had ever penetrated into Germany.

Then Caesar showed wise statesmanship. Instead
of advancing in depth, he withdrew. He knew that
the time was not ripe for a full-scale invasion of
Germany. All he wanted to do just then was to
prove his strength and teach the Germans who was

master. He wanted to make it clear to them that they must keep out of France and the Low Countries, no matter what.

Caesar, in other words, decided that the Rhine should be Germany's western frontier. It is still the frontier today.

Extraordinary feats of heroism took place on both sides during the Gallic wars. Here is Caesar's own

account of an incident in a battle against the
Germans:

In this engagement seventy-four of our cavalry-
men were killed, including Piso, a gallant Aqui-
tanian of very good family, whose grandfather
had been king of his tribe and had been granted
the title of "Friend" by the Roman Senate. He
went to the assistance of his brother, who was
cut off by some of the Germans, and succeeded
in rescuing him; but his own horse was wounded
and threw him. As long as he could, he resisted
with the utmost bravery, but eventually was surrounded and fell covered with wounds. When
his brother, who by this time had got well away
from the fight, saw what had happened, he
galloped straight up to the enemy and let them
kill him too.

Another episode which took place later in the
siege of a town in Belgium is described by Caesar
as follows:

There was a Gaul standing before one of the
gates and throwing into the flames, opposite one
of our towers, lumps of tallow and pitch that were
passed along to him. An arrow from a catapult

pierced his right side and he fell dead. Another near him stepped over his prostrate body and took over his job. When he likewise was killed by the catapult, a third took his place, and so they went on. The post was not abandoned by the defenders until the fire on the terrace was extinguished, the Gauls repulsed all along the line, and the battle at an end.*

After the German invasion Caesar made two remarkable forays into Britain, first in the year 55 B.C. and then, with more strength, the following year. To build a fleet, cross the stormy English Channel, and invade Britain was a terrifically bold and adventurous thing to do. Several motives prompted Caesar. One was probably simple curiosity. Another was the belief that unknown Britain was fabulously rich in such commodities as pearls and tin. Still another sprang from military considerations. Caesar thought that the British might, in time, lend assistance to the Gauls, and he wanted to protect his northern flank.

The first invasion was only a reconnaissance. Caesar prodded into Kent, then withdrew. But when he returned the next year he brought a big

* From Caesar, *The Conquest of Gaul,* translated by S. A. Hanford, Penguin Classics, 1951.

army with him—five legions—and stayed several
months. He found the Britons, then as now, to be
hard fighters in defense of their freedom and their
native land. Also, daubed with blue dye and riding
in extraordinary armed chariots, they put up a
splendid, terrifying show.

Caesar won several battles, and got a fair way in-
land. Probably he was the first important Italian
ever to sleep in what is now London. But he knew
that it would cost him too much to stay. Storms
played havoc with his fleet, and he could not risk
further loss to his ships. So he returned to France,
with a few hostages and a small amount of booty.

By this time Caesar's technique as a soldier was
established. For one thing he was, as a contemporary military expert puts it, "an unsurpassed master
of the art of quick maneuver." Few generals in
history have been so capable of moving large
forces so swiftly. Caesar never fought unless he

was in a good position to win, and, what is more, he always contrived to establish such a position. Almost never did he take a risk.

Nor was that all. As well as being intelligent, Caesar was always full of common sense. Plenty of great men have been intelligent, but not all of them showed common sense.

Then, like almost all good generals, Caesar pre-

ferred peace to war. If he could win a result without fighting, he didn't fight.

He could, however, be absolutely ruthless if he
thought that ruthlessness was necessary. Once,
toward the end of the Gallic campaigns, a tribe
broke its word and revolted. Caesar sacked its
chief city and, as he himself wrote with chill-
ing blandness, ordered that *the hands of every
man who had fought against him be cut off.*
Handless, these pitiable and wretched creatures
were released so that, in Caesar's own words,
"Everyone might see what punishment was meted
out to evildoers."

Caesar built up a remarkable morale in his own
army. His men loved him, and would follow him
to the death. He drove them hard, but he also rewarded them well. He let discipline be relaxed
when they were not in contact with the enemy, and
they had plenty of leisure between marches. They
received high pay, and were often given slaves as
loot.

Somebody complained to him once, after his
men had taken a town and had done some looting,
that they smelled of perfume. Caesar replied dryly
that they would fight well no matter how they
smelled.

He kept his troops constantly on the alert if the

enemy was near, and was forever testing them. He would make them work in bad weather or on holidays if action was impending. Sometimes, as an exercise, he himself would disappear for days and search parties would have the task of tracking him down and finding him.

In one early battle his men seemed frightened. Caesar at once had all the horses in the whole army, including his own, put away out of sight. His men understood quickly; everybody was going to be equally exposed to danger, and nobody would be able to run away.

One reason why he was so beloved was that he had stamina as well as courage. His example made his men invincible. Caesar marched in the ranks with his troops, slept with them, ate with them, and shared their hardships. If food was short, he didn't eat.

He never gave a thought to danger. Once he dressed himself up as a Gaul and penetrated the enemy's lines in disguise in order to verify information brought in by his scouts. Another time, when his cavalry was held up, he dismounted at the head of his men and led the attack on foot. In the great battle against the Nervii all the centurions in a cohort were killed. Caesar, who was not even wearing a shield, grabbed one from the nearest

soldier and went into the front line to lead his men.

The Gauls came to respect him too. Before the end of the war he recruited and put into action a legion composed entirely of Gauls, called the Lark.

Caesar had the help of several able subordinates, whom he trained. One, the son of Crassus, saved the day for him in a battle which he came close to losing. Another was Titus Labienus, who had been his right-hand man for years. Still another, Cicero's brother, did well in various battles. One more, Decimus Brutus, was his best naval officer. Caesar was very fond of him.

Gaul was fairly quiet during the years 54 B.C. and 53 B.C. Then there was an uprising by a king named Ambiorix, in the Ardennes. It was a bitter fight, but Caesar vanquished him. It seemed that the long, arduous Gallic war was over.

But it wasn't.

❦ XII ❦

The Last Act in Gaul

Caesar's most difficult and dangerous campaign in
Gaul was still ahead of him. What made it necessary was an uprising in 52 B.C. by a great Gallic
patriot and military chieftain, Vercingetorix. A tall,
blond man with long hair and a shaggy beard,
Vercingetorix was a nobleman, the son of a king,
and leader of the Avernians. Proud and courageous,
he was the ablest military man the Gauls ever
produced.

Vercingetorix succeeded in raising almost all of
Gaul against Caesar, who was caught by surprise.
The revolt was well organized, and spread like
wildfire, for the people clung steadfastly to their
leader's side. Vercingetorix was a stubborn fighter,
and it seemed that all of Caesar's work in the past
years might go down in ruins.

Vercingetorix was full of tricks. For instance, he displayed a sword which he said had been captured from Caesar, and hung it up in a temple in the chief town of the Avernians. This impressed his superstitious people mightily, although it was not true that the sword, an ordinary Roman sword, had ever actually belonged to Caesar.

Now it was winter. Caesar marshalled his hard-pressed legions, which performed unheard-of feats cutting paths through the heavy snow that still clung to the mountains. He gave pursuit to Vercingetorix, and several tumultuous battles were fought without decisive result.

Vercingetorix had 300,000 warriors. He reached Alexia, a hill town in Burgundy that was strongly fortified. Caesar set out to besiege him, and the Romans built massive walls and towers and dug deep trenches. Then Caesar surrounded Alexia with his best troops, with the idea of starving out the Gauls. But other Gallic hordes marched to relieve Vercingetorix, and soon Caesar found that *his* armies were surrounded. There were two concentric rings of troops around Alexia, and Caesar was caught between two fires.

Even so, his generalship won the day. The ring of Gauls encircling Caesar was broken up and then the Romans, using complex and efficient siege ma-

chinery, increased their pressure on the town. Finally the helpless Vercingetorix, with his food supply gone and his people starving, was forced to surrender.

The gates of Alexia opened. Vercingetorix, with as much dignity as any Roman, rode out of the conquered city on a horse decked with rich spangles and blankets. Caesar awaited him sternly in a chair of state outside the city walls, and Vercingetorix approached. His men threw down their weapons, and Vercingetorix, saying not a word, disdaining to appeal for mercy, dismounted and prostrated himself before the Roman victor. Caesar hesitated for a moment, not knowing what to do with this brave, proud adversary. Then he ordered him to be put away in chains.

Vercingetorix was transported down to Rome, where he languished in prison until, years later, Caesar used him as an ornament in one of his triumphs. At the end Vercingetorix was strangled in a dungeon under the Roman capitol—an unseemly fate for such a gallant man.

After the defeat of Vercingetorix, Gaul was quiet. The great Gallic war was over, and Caesar busied himself by consolidating his victories and transforming Gaul into a stable, friendly Roman dominion.

With his great accomplishments in Gaul Caesar proved himself to be one of the foremost soldiers in history. This is particularly noteworthy because he had never led large bodies of troops before he arrived in Gaul in 58 B.C., when he was already in his forties. Napoleon became immortal as a successful general before he was thirty, but not Caesar. Caesar had done a bit of fighting in the East as a youth and had commanded a minor army in Spain, but otherwise he was completely without professional experience. He had no regular training as an officer at all.

Another extraordinary point is that during the nine long years he fought in Gaul, Caesar was never wounded. Alexander the Great was badly wounded several times in the course of his campaigns, but Caesar, although he often stood in the forefront of his troops, sharing the common infantryman's duties, never got a scratch.

In nine years Caesar doubled the size of the Rome territories, and opened up, subdued, and gave organization to lands much bigger than Italy itself. He took eight hundred towns and cities, conquered three hundred small nations, fought fifty battles, and defeated roughly three million enemy troops.

This is a good time to have a brief additional

word about Caesar's character. This was full of con-
tradictions, and even today, two thousand years
later, is still something of an enigma to those who
study him.

Consider how differently he has been viewed by
various writers. Shakespeare makes him seem
touchy, tired, and arrogant, although Shakespeare
has Mark Antony call him "the noblest man that
ever lived in the tide of times."

Shaw, in *Caesar and Cleopatra,* portrays him as
being wonderfully wise, humorous, clever, tolerant,
and seasoned. A great German historian says that
"he was the sole creative genius produced by
Rome." But some contemporary authorities call
him an "aristocratic egoist" and "Fascist."

Everybody will agree that his name, right down
to today, symbolizes authority and majesty. The
titles "Czar" and "Kaiser" both come from "Caesar." The name even appeared in the British royal
title for many years, because the British monarch
was called "Kaiser-i-Hind," or Emperor of India,
until recently.

One of Caesar's characteristics was, beyond doubt,
gentlemanliness. He certainly did unpleasant things
on occasion, but there was no trace of vulgarity in
Caesar. He was a true aristocrat, and had true
style.

He had an exceptionally rational mind. He was logical, a realist. He believed in results, not theories. He was intensely sophisticated, and he loved subtlety.

In most personal habits he was abstemious, even austere. He hated useless display in his later years and he became puritanical about luxuries as he grew older. He had iron self-control and self-discipline.

Another outstanding characteristic was his ability to work hard, his diligence. Moreover he was versatile, and did well at almost anything he tried, from oratory to winning battles. His memory was remarkable. One historian records that he could use his eyes, ears, hands, and mind at the same time. That is, he could read a report, listen to an advisor, dictate a memorandum, and think about the future all at once.

There are a good many things to say on the debit side. He was often guilty of disreputable behavior, particularly when he was young, and he was sometimes cruel. He would do almost anything to get ahead, and he was always inclined to be unscrupulous about money. One contemporary says that he was a pronounced hypocrite, who "kissed his enemies after they were dead."

He was loved by his troops, but he did not have

many close personal friends. He had an air of
inhumanity about him. Moreover several of his
closest friends betrayed him in the end, like his best
general, Titus Labienus.

He was, of course, fantastically ambitious, as
well as one of the cleverest men who ever lived.
It was his ambition and super-cleverness that ruined
him before many more years passed. He never
built up a body of close associates based on faith.
Nobody quite trusted him, which is one of the most
damaging things that can ever happen to a man.

There were two things Caesar believed in above
all—efficiency, and himself.

❦ XIII ❦

The Rubicon

Now, in 51 B.C., Caesar's term in Gaul would soon expire. But the Triumvirate had blown up for a variety of reasons, and Rome was in a state of virtual chaos. Caesar had to make the great decision of his life—whether or not to impose his own will on the Roman state by force.

Meantime, he took stock of his personal relationships. His immediate family had dwindled. There were left now only Calpurnia, his sisters, and his grandnephew Octavius. His mother died while he was absent in Gaul, as had his only grandson, the infant son of Pompey and Julia. And Julia herself had died in childbirth. This served to weaken the relationship between Pompey and Caesar, which had become strained again.

True, Caesar did his best to patch things up. He

suggested that Pompey should marry a lady named
Octavia, who was his sister's granddaughter. She
was already married, but it would have been easy
enough to arrange a divorce. But Pompey refused
this offer.

Caesar, it appears, then even went so far as to
offer to divorce his own wife, Calpurnia, in order
to marry one of Pompey's daughters. But this idea
fell through as well.

As for Crassus, he had been killed in Asia in the
year 53 B.C. He had marched beyond his own province
of Syria to attack a savage country, Parthia, which
lay farther to the east. He wanted to outdo Caesar
in extending the boundaries of Rome. But he was
defeated in battle and lost his life ignominiously. So
this rich man met his end.

With Crassus gone, relations between Caesar
and Pompey became tense. Crassus had been a
kind of buffer between them, but now they were
"at jar" with one another. Pompey then married
Crassus's widow, astonishingly enough, partly as a
maneuver against Caesar.

Then came another death which played a role in
Caesar's fortunes. Caesar had been counting on
Clodius, the young ruffian whom he had made a
tribune, to control the Senate for him and, if necessary, put pressure on the government by inciting

the mob and making trouble on the streets. But Clodius was killed in a fight with members of a rival
gang set up by Pompey.

The situation in Rome became bewilderingly
complicated. Rioters burned down the Senate.
Pompey, frightened, sought to work harmoniously
with Caesar for a time, but then, reaching for supreme power himself, became hostile again. It
was clear that, unless some miracle intervened,
Caesar and Pompey would have to fight it out, and
might destroy each other.

The great orator Cicero, who had been deeply
impressed by Caesar's final victories in Gaul and
was now friendly to him, tried to patch things up.
But Cicero's influence, despite his eloquent speech-
making, was not powerful enough to count.

Pompey became sole consul—that is, virtual dictator—for a year, and threw in his hand with the
Optimates in the Senate. Here were Caesar's
bitterest enemies. They now decided to try to deprive him of his command, drag him back to
Rome, and put him on trial for various "crimes."

Caesar watched these developments closely. The
dates were vitally important, and time was getting
short. Caesar was invulnerable so long as he stayed
out of Italy and retained his command. But this
would expire sometime in 49 b.c., and he could not

legally be elected consul, when he would be automatically immune from prosecution, until the following year.

So, to fill the gap, he sought to get his command extended. Pompey took up an attitude of pious neutrality about this, and Caesar's request was turned down by the Senate.

Even now, Caesar hoped to avoid civil war between Pompey and himself, and he made several conciliatory offers to Pompey and the Senate. They were all refused. Finally he said that he would disband his army if Pompey would disband his.

At Ravenna, Caesar waited for a reply to this new offer. A furious debate took place in the Senate. Caesar's old enemy Cato, supported by a tiny clique of extreme reactionaries, was determined to bring Caesar to ruin. Caesar's Populares were voted down, the tribunes of the people were attacked, and the upshot was that Caesar, but not Pompey, was ordered to give up his command and lay down his arms by a certain date. If not, he would be declared a public enemy.

Mark Antony rushed up to Ravenna with this appalling news. Caesar's opponents were fixed in their determination to destroy him.

Caesar pondered, and then decided to take action at once. He would march on Rome. It was by far the most critical and agonizing decision of his life. He knew that if he went forward, civil war would inevitably follow; moreover, that events would almost certainly compel him to be dictator.

What he was going to do, if he did it, would destroy the Roman republic. Yet if he did not do it his own career and life were certainly doomed. Besides, he was a patriot and he thought that it was absolutely in the public interest that he should march on Rome in order to save it from anarchy.

The Rubicon, an inconspicuous river, formed the southern boundary of Caesar's command. With a small group of friends, Caesar strolled down from his camp at dusk to look at it, wondering what course events would take. The water was brown and muddy—it was not a very impressive-looking stream. Yet it held his fate.

Once the Rubicon was crossed, Caesar would be a public enemy, fighting for his very existence. This he knew well. He grasped one of his lieutenants by the arm and, sighing, uttered the exclamation, "Well! A man can only be undone once!" He returned to his camp, and that night had a strange and terrifying dream in which he was hitting his own mother.

The next day, a bright January morning in 49 B.C., with all doubts behind him, he marched with

a small detachment to cross the Rubicon. He was firm and confident. The man closest to his side was Mark Antony.

Legend has it that awesome apparitions appeared on the southern bank of the Rubicon as Caesar trod across. Flames shot up in the sky, and the gods moaned. But Caesar paid no attention, and went forward swiftly. He shouted to his men, "The die is cast!"

PART III

❧ XIV ❧

The Civil War

Caesar's army numbered about fifty thousand men. Pompey had many more, and so Caesar was at a disadvantage when the civil war began. Moreover, Pompey's military prestige was still greater than Caesar's, in spite of Caesar's imposing victories in Gaul. The handsome Pompey had troops all over the world and, in his whole history as a military commander, had never lost a battle.

Nevertheless Caesar beat him easily in the first campaign, and took all of Italy in the astounding time of six weeks. Actually, very little fighting took place. People simply fled before the threat of Caesar's advance. Cities emptied themselves. Caesar entered Rome in a walk, and the frightened Senate named him dictator. But he resigned the dictatorship after eleven days, and had himself made consul, which had been his original design.

The splendid Pompey, not so splendid now, fled to Greece. To everybody's surprise, Caesar did not pursue him there at once, but went to Spain instead. The reason was that he wanted to protect his western flank. Two of Pompey's best subordinates held commands in Spain, and Caesar would not be safe until he got rid of them.

Caesar's campaign in Spain was short. It was one of the most brilliant he ever fought, and almost bloodless. Spain fell into his outspread arms.

One interesting thing was that, during this campaign, Gaul remained perfectly quiet. The Gauls could easily have taken advantage of the uproar in Rome and the civil strife between Caesar and Pompey to make a revolt, but they did not do so. They were cowed, for one thing. Also Caesar had done a lot in his last years in Gaul to heal the wounds of the Gallic war. With masterly statesmanship, he had given the Gauls important concessions, and made them feel that they were proud partners in the Roman state.

Confident of the outcome in Spain and impatient to get on to other tasks, Caesar left Spain before the fighting was over and returned to Rome. Several of his best generals, among them Decimus Brutus, remained behind to clean up. Decimus Brutus took Marseilles in a naval action, and not long after the islands of Sicily and Sardinia went over to Caesar's men.

Soon it came time for Caesar to prepare for fighting Pompey in Greece. Caesar still had a good deal of respect for Pompey, and had been deeply fond of him as a man. But now he made light of Pompey's military position. With his flashing, ironic smile, he said: "In Spain I beat an army without a general, and now I will go to Greece to beat a general without an army."

Caesar took no repressive measures in Rome. He didn't punish anybody. Some people thought that he would make a general massacre of his enemies, but nothing of the sort happened. Caesar remembered the horrors of the proscriptions when Sulla had seized Rome, and he was determined to let nothing of the sort occur again. He wanted, at this time, to be as legal a ruler as possible, and he distinguished himself for his mildness and reasonable behavior.

Once, however, when Metellus, one of the tribunes, sought to oppose him, Caesar said simply, "If you trouble me any more, I will have you killed." Then he added, half-humorously, "You know, it is much harder for me to tell you this than to put the order into execution!" Metellus gave him no further trouble.

When it became known that Caesar, in the dead of winter, planned to set out for Greece and the East on a new, dangerous, and difficult campaign, some of his troops protested. In spite of the immense rewards he had given them, they were sick and tired of fighting. Caesar's reply was characteristic. He set sail across the Adriatic anyway with a small detachment, and soon his legions, even if they were grumbling and discontented, dutifully followed him.

He gained a foothold on the other side of the Adriatic, but soon encountered serious delays in getting reinforcements and supplies. He decided to make a quick trip back to Italy to see what the situation was. But there were no warships available, and in the teeth of a fierce wintry gale he had to take a small sailing vessel. The captain was afraid to sail. Caesar reassured him with the words, "Be of good cheer. Nothing can possibly happen to you, because you are carrying Caesar and his fortunes!"

The campaign against Pompey in Greece was bitterly difficult. Caesar did not relish the idea of civil war and of killing fellow Romans, and he made Pompey several honorable offers of peace. He said to one of his companions sadly, "The war is Pompey's doing. I fight against my own will."

Fighting aside, Caesar was delighted to be in

Greece. From his boyhood days he had loved Greek culture. He had steeped himself for years in Greek language, Greek art, and Greek philosophy. So he made elaborate plans to revive the former glories of Greece, now in decay, and to improve economic conditions in the country.

Meanwhile, his men were ill fed. Pompey controlled the seas and blockaded the Adriatic so that provisions could not reach Caesar. The Caesar legions, all but starving, were reduced to eating grass and reeds. Pompey, hearing of this, exclaimed with contempt, "What! Are these animals that I am fighting?"

Then Caesar's troops fell victim to an ugly epidemic caused by eating bad meat. They cured themselves at last by drinking colossal quantities of wine, which apparently had the effect of combatting the mysterious infection. Pompey, when his spies told him this, was amazed. Luck always seemed to be on Caesar's side.

Pompey was entrenched at Dyrrhachium, which is the modern town of Durazzo, in Albania. Caesar tried to take this citadel by storm, but failed. The battle was so fierce that 130,000 arrows were picked up off the field later. Caesar said that if Pompey had been resolute enough to follow up his advantage at Dyrrhachium, he might have won the war. He commented dryly, "Pompey is a general who knows how to win battles, but not wars."

Then, in 48 B.C., came Pharsalus, one of the great decisive battles of the world. Oddly enough, the exact spot where this celebrated engagement took place in Thessaly (Thrace) has never been identified.

The night before the battle a spectacular meteor, or "firebrant," burst over the sky. It rose over Caesar's camp, and then fell down in Pompey's. This, the soothsayers said, meant that Caesar was bound to win, and his troops were much encouraged. Anyway Caesar won, and his victory was overwhelming.

The battle, a classic of ancient military art, is still studied in academies like West Point.

Caesar won mostly as a result of careful, subtle planning. He anchored his troops on a small river, to protect his left flank. Then he enticed Pompey to attack on the right, where he had his heavy cohorts concealed by a screen of cavalry. Pompey fell into this trap, and Caesar, releasing his hidden reserves at exactly the right moment, was able to sweep forward and surround most of Pompey's men. The heavy legions punched a hole through Pompey's center, and the cavalry cut off his flanks.

Another reason for Caesar's victory was that he used his knowledge of human nature against the enemy. He told his javelin throwers to aim at the faces of the enemy, not at their bodies as was the usual custom, and moreover to use their javelins as daggers at close range, not as spears. Caesar knew that Pompey's best troops were fashionable young Romans who would hate to have their faces scarred. He was right. They ran away.

Word was brought to Pompey that all was lost, and that Caesar's troops were close at hand. "What! In my very camp!" exclaimed Pompey, heartbroken and not believing that such dire news could be true. Then he fled.

Caesar took several important prisoners at Pharsalus, among them a Roman of good family named Marcus Brutus, who was famous for his nobility of character. Caesar had known Brutus for many years, and had been deeply hurt and disappointed when Brutus went over to Pompey's side. Caesar not only saved Brutus's life after Pharsalus, but forgave him. History might have been very different if he had not done so.

Pompey escaped with remnants of his routed army, and made his way to Egypt. There was nothing else for him to do. Perhaps he thought that in Egypt or Asia he might recoup his fortunes, for he still had many supporters scattered through the world. But it was not to be. Soon after his arrival in Egypt he was treacherously assassinated. The Egyptians killed him thinking that this would improve their position with the victorious Caesar.

When Caesar arrived in Egypt a little later the Egyptian monarch proudly presented him with the head of Pompey. But Caesar was not pleased at all. He covered his eyes sorrowfully and commanded, "Take it away. I will not look at it."

So ended the first phase of the civil war. Caesar had time to pause.

❦ XV ❦

Cleopatra—and After

Arriving in Egypt in the full glory of success, Caesar soon met Cleopatra, the youthful Egyptian queen. She was one of the most fascinating women who ever lived, and Caesar promptly fell victim to her spell, although he was in his fifties now and she was under twenty.

Oddly enough Cleopatra was not Egyptian at all, although she claimed descent from the old Egyptian gods. In fact she was a pure-blooded Macedonian Greek. A Greek dynasty had been ruling Egypt since the times of Alexander the Great centuries before, and the youthful Cleopatra, "last of the Ptolemies," was a member of this line.

She ruled Egypt jointly with her brother, Ptolemy XII, who was a boy of thirteen. But Cleopatra and her brother did not get along well, and when Caesar arrived in Egypt they were continually squabbling and intriguing against each other.

Caesar met Cleopatra for the first time in her palace at Alexandria, and was deeply impressed not only by her beauty but also by her knowledge of statecraft.

Cleopatra was marvelously attractive. This was not merely on account of her looks. She had great charm as well, an exceptionally pleasant voice, and was full of sweetness and grace—so at least the old chroniclers say. (Also, of course, she could be as cruel as a viper.) She liked to talk, knew seven languages, and had an original, lively mind. She learned things fast, and was an accomplished politician. Like many Greeks, she was apt to be very quick in changing her emotions; she could be gay one moment, mischievous the next, and stately and queenlike the next. She was at once fierce, kittenish and tender. Shakespeare characterized her thus:

Age cannot wither her, nor custom stale
Her infinite variety: other women cloy
The appetites they feed, but she makes hungry,
Where most she satisfies.

Egypt was not part of the Roman state at this time, but, for a variety of reasons, a small Roman garrison was stationed at Alexandria. This was under the command of a man named Achillas.

Caesar had come to Egypt for several reasons. First, Egypt interested him very much. He had had his eye on this country, with its magnificent old history and splendid wealth, for many years. Second, it was his duty to pursue and get rid of the remnant of Pompey's forces which had arrived in Egypt. Third, Egypt owed Rome a lot of money, which Caesar wanted to collect.

Caesar felt that it was safe for him to stay away from Rome for some time. For one thing, he had left Mark Antony behind, as his deputy or Master of the Horse, to watch his interests. For another, he foresaw no immediate trouble with the Senate. Indeed, now that Pompey was gone, the Senate wanted to curry favor with the new master, and heaped honor after honor on Caesar's head.

One day a courier arrived from Thessaly with a bag containing all of Pompey's secret papers. It had been found in Pompey's camp at Pharsalus. The papers contained the name of every man in Rome who was a spy, an agent, or a secret enemy against Caesar. With this evidence it would be easy for him to get rid of all these opponents. But without even opening the bag Caesar calmly ordered it to be destroyed. His lieutenants were astounded, but by this

act Caesar made it clear he did not seek revenge.

Egypt, then as now, was a country full of intrigue. The most important political personality was a sinister creature named Pothinus. From the beginning he made trouble for Caesar. His first move was to drive Cleopatra out into the desert, away from the court, so that he could have a free hand for his dealing against Caesar, whom he hated.

Pothinus tried to stir up unrest by giving Caesar's soldiers bad food. Caesar summoned Pothinus into his presence, told him that he would take no more nonsense from him, and demanded a very large sum as tribute. Pothinus had to accept Caesar's terms. But, surreptitiously, he began to foment a civil war in order to embarrass Caesar. He gained the assistance of the Roman general Achillas, and then sought to make use of Cleopatra's brother Ptolemy, who hated her.

Caesar got wind of this plot. His first move was to protect Cleopatra. He could not summon her openly, for she might be intercepted and killed. So she came to him stealthily, by secret means, and was delivered to his headquarters hidden in a pile of rugs.

Caesar's idea was to heal the quarrel between Cleopatra and young Ptolemy, so that brother and sister might rule together peaceably. Again, Pothinus sought to interfere. A slave who was Caesar's barber told Caesar about the new plot: A sumptuous banquet was being prepared for that night, at which Caesar would be poisoned. Enraged, Caesar waited till Pothinus arrived at the banquet, and then slew him with his own hand.

Now war did break out. It was a confusing and unpleasant little war. Achillas rose against Caesar, allying himself with the Egyptians under young Ptolemy. Caesar had brought very few troops with him to Egypt, and he was seriously outnumbered. He was forced to retire to an isolated group of buildings, and was besieged near the waterfront. His troops suffered severely from a shortage of drinking water. During the fighting the great Alexandria library was burned down by accident, and the world lost an irreplaceable treasure.

Caesar had one narrow escape. Fighting near the Alexandria lighthouse, he thought that he could get at the enemy better by taking to a boat. But the boat was tipped over by the Egyptian forces, and Caesar, to save himself, had to swim to the nearest refuge. Arrows fell near him so thick and fast that he had to duck between strokes. Also he had to manage to keep one hand above the water, because he was carrying some important state papers and he did not want them to be damaged or lost.

Caesar won the Egyptian war in good time, and
his enemies dispersed. Young Ptolemy was killed in
battle. Caesar, triumphant and relaxed, spent several
months in Cleopatra's company. They took a long,
pleasant trip down the Nile on a magnificently decorated barge, at the head of a fleet of a dozen splendid vessels which carried musicians, entertainers, and
the like. This was the first holiday Caesar had had
in many years, and he enjoyed it thoroughly.

Caesar and the pleasure-loving Cleopatra might
have gone all the way to Ethiopia, as Caesar wanted
to do, if his troops had not become restless. They
threatened to make trouble if he did not return to
Alexandria. Reluctantly he did so.

Now it came time for him to resume his campaigns. There was serious business to deal with in
the East. Caesar told Cleopatra that he would have
to depart from her for the time being, and they said
a sad, affectionate farewell.

Caesar's prestige had reached immense propor-
tions by this time. And his joy in Cleopatra's glow-
ing talents and beauty gave him a new spurt in creative energy. He was like a man possessed.

He set out to cross the Hellespont in a small naval
craft, and saw bearing down on him a fleet of ten
large warships commanded by one of Pompey's
lieutenants, Lucius Cassius. Caesar made not the

slightest attempt to get away, although he was over-whelmingly outnumbered. Instead, defiantly, he rowed up to Cassius' flagship and demanded *his* surrender! What is more, the awed Cassius at once surrendered.

Then came the battle of Zela. A son of the great Asiatic chieftain Mithridates, who had made so much trouble for Rome in Caesar's youth, rose against Roman dominion in the region beyond Syria. His name was Pharnaces. Caesar had only three legions. Nevertheless he marched quickly against Pharnaces, and beat him handily at a town called Zela. Perhaps this battle did not amount to much in itself, but it was to become forever associated with one of the most famous messages ever sent by a military commander anywhere. Caesar always liked to be brief and to the point. Now he outdid himself. Announcing his victory to the Senate in Rome, he restricted himself to three words: *"Veni, Vidi, Vici."* But what a wealth of meaning in those three words! "I came, I saw, I conquered."

✿ XVI ✿

Battles in Africa and Spain

At last Caesar returned to Rome. It was now 47 B.C., and he had been away for almost two years. Rome exploded with demonstrations of thanksgiving. The great and immortal Caesar was home again!

However, signs of discontent at Caesar's methods of rule were beginning to be evident. Some of his best men became disgruntled. There was a growing fear that he was overreaching himself and would soon destroy the old Rome by making himself permanent ruler, or even king. There were thousands upon thousands of good Romans who were still solidly loyal to the ideals of the old, self-governing republic, although in truth the republic had lost many of its ideals and was inefficient and corrupt.

At this time an unpleasant and unexpected thing happened. There was a mutiny in Caesar's favorite legion, the Tenth. His veterans went wild on the streets of Rome, looting and murdering. The excuse for this is that even the best of troops get tired sometimes. Men of the Tenth had been fighting practically without interruption for more than a decade. They wanted to retire from the army, get farms out in the countryside, and say goodbye to battle, blood, and pestilence.

Caesar dealt with this threat in his usual confident way. He summoned the mutinous centurions together, and instead of using the word "comrades," as he usually did on such occasions, he called these battle-worn veterans "civilians," in a tone of utter contempt. Humiliated, they denied that they were civilians, and asked to be accepted as soldiers once again. The clever Caesar was only too glad to comply with this request. He did not punish the mutineers but, on the contrary, gave them $1,000 each and promised them new land.

Caesar learned a lesson from this episode: it was necessary not merely to give his troops ample rewards, but to keep them busy all the time. At this time Caesar had about thirty-two legions in all. From then on he always kept about twenty-five of these stationed on active duty on some remote frontier.

Now a dangerous situation arose in Africa which

challenged Caesar's best attention. Pompey was dead
and Caesar had full power *in Rome*, but many of
the old Pompey people—the nobles, members of
the Optimate party, and other reactionaries—still
refused stubbornly to accept Caesar's rule. They
were determined to fight him to the death. They
fled to the North African coast and collected a large
army there, a bigger one than Caesar had. Their
leaders were the stony Cato, who was still the re-
lentless, implacable foe of Caesar, and a distinguished officer named Metellus Scipio. Moreover
they succeeded in getting the local ruler, King
Juba of Numidia, to join them and fight on their
side.

Caesar encountered grave difficulties. He took to
the sea with three thousand men, but raging storms
scattered his fleet. At last he landed at a lonely beach
in what is now Tunisia, near the town of Sfax. Caesar,
at the head of his men, slipped in the wet sand and
fell headlong. Quickly he recovered himself, and, so
as not to seem lacking in dignity as a result of the
fall, pretended to be kneeling and embracing the
African soil as a good-luck gesture to his troops.
Kissing the wet sand, he called out loudly, "I hold
thee fast, Africa!"

Metellus Scipio, the chief commander against
Caesar, was descended from one of the most cele-

brated of all Roman soldiers, Scipio Africanus, who
had won everlasting fame in the Punic Wars. And
there was a legend, believed in devoutly by the
superstitious Romans, that nobody named Scipio
could ever be beaten in a battle in Africa. Caesar
at once worked out a stratagem to counteract this
superstition. He found *another* man named Scipio,
an obscure officer on his staff, and gave him an important position. So, with a Scipio on *his* side, he
could not be beaten, either!

The Numidians were excellent soldiers, particularly as light horsemen, and they played havoc with
Caesar's flanks as he advanced. His men became
nervous. Rumors spread that King Juba had such a
large force that he would be impossible to beat.
Caesar called his troops together, and addressed
them with calm irony. "I understand that King Juba
has two million men and two thousand elephants,"
he said. "Now you know the facts as well as I do.
I suppose you're frightened to death. If so, leave
my army and go back to Rome, and I'll deal with
Juba all by myself."

Caesar's gibe worked. His men promptly regained
their morale, and went into action with pride and
daring.

Even so, the African campaign was difficult.
Caesar's men were so short of food that they had

to eat seaweed, which made them sick. Caesar himself saved the day in one fierce skirmish with Juba's men. One of his most trusted standard bearers became panicky at the climax of the battle, turned, and fled from the enemy. His troops wavered. Caesar, furious, grabbed the standard himself and strode forward with it. "This way!" he shouted. "Your enemies are in front, not in back!"

The decisive battle was fought at Thapsus in 46 B.C. This was near the site of ancient Carthage. Caesar showed masterful strategy, as usual. He was weak in cavalry, and the Numidian horsemen were dangerous. So Caesar contrived to have the battle take place on a narrow spit of land where the enemy cavalry had no room to maneuver. He was taking a terrible risk, because if he was beaten he would have no avenue of escape. But his gamble paid off, and he won a signal victory. Fifty thousand of the enemy were killed, and his own losses totaled only fifty.

He did not, however, take part in this great battle himself. He planned and directed it, but did not do any of the fighting. This was because he had had a sudden stroke of "falling sickness," or epilepsy, the night before.

Caesar's formidable enemy Cato killed himself after his utter defeat in this battle. He was a real

Roman to the end. Caesar went to see the body in the enemy's camp, and was shocked and saddened.

Then came Caesar's last campaign. It took place in Spain, where two of Pompey's sons, who had taken refuge there, rose against him. Caesar thought that he had thoroughly pacified Spain at the beginning of the civil war, but events now proved him wrong.

Titus Labienus, for many years Caesar's closest comrade and best soldier, had gone over to the enemy, and was now a leader of the Pompey forces. He was thoroughly familiar with all of Caesar's tricks, and knew exactly how his former commander liked to fight a battle. So Caesar had to be doubly careful.

The Spanish war, Caesar's last, was the hardest since the campaign against Vercingetorix, even though many of the Pompeyite troops were youthful and inexperienced. The decisive battle took place at Munda, not far from Seville. Caesar won, but the outcome was doubtful until the eleventh hour. Caesar himself led the final charge on foot, uphill, as the sun was setting. He cheered his veterans on by shouting, "What! Aren't you ashamed, my men from many battles, to be beaten and taken prisoner by these young boys?"

This was the first battle Caesar had ever fought in which his own life was in serious danger. At

Munda he was fighting not merely for victory, but for survival. If he had been beaten, he told his friends later, he would have committed suicide.

In this battle Caesar gave his youthful grand-nephew Octavius his first taste of blood. Octavius fought by Caesar's side, and acquitted himself very well.

After the victory at Munda, Caesar returned to Rome. He was now undisputed master of the whole Mediterranean world, and held more power in his hands, all the way from the English Channel to the borders of Parthia near the Euphrates, than any conqueror in history.

🏵 XVII 🏵

Back in Rome

Time began to run out for Caesar now, despite his victories. But first he tasted glories such as no Roman has ever known before or since.

Already, in the interval between Thapsus and Munda, prodigious festivities had taken place. Caesar was granted not merely one triumph, but three —one for Egypt, one for Zela ("I came, I saw, I conquered") and one for North Africa. Later came two more. A far cry from the time in his early days when the Senate had refused to let him have any triumph at all!

He had plenty of money to spend now, since the spoils he had picked up were beyond expectation. Once more he rewarded his troops with royal extravagance, and put on magnificent games and circuses for the people at large. He arranged to have a mock naval battle fought in the Tiber, with whole fleets participating. He gave a sumptuous feast in memory of his daughter Julia, at which citizens were served at no fewer than twenty-two *thousand* tables.

But not all of the people of Rome were favorably disposed toward him. Many deplored such excesses. At one mass meeting which Caesar summoned, expecting a crowd of 320,000, only about 150,000 men and women appeared. Whispers mounted that Caesar had gone too far, and many good Romans were mourning sons killed in the long years of bloodshed and civil war.

Politically, however, he was strong enough at the moment to have everything his own way. Caesar, like most men in high positions reached by irregular means, sought to "institutionalize" himself; that is, to make his rule legal and respectable.

After the victory over Pompey at Pharsalus he had been appointed Dictator for the second time. The length of the term was not defined. Then, in 46 B.C., he was elected to a third dictatorship which was to last for ten whole years. Meantime, he served four different terms as consul, and was also a tribune. The post of tribune was important because, in theory, a tribune could veto legislation and his person was sacred from assault. Moreover, during all this time, he had held on to his old title of Ponti-

fex Maximus. This too gave him added prestige by
stressing his religious functions and giving him further immunity against attack. A lot of people might
throw a rock at a consul or even a tribune, but to
attempt violence on the body of a Pontifex Maximus
was an extremely grave offense. Finally, Caesar was
the first person in Roman history to get the *permanent* title of Imperator—literally, "Victorious General."

Again, there were plenty of Romans who disap-
proved vigorously of such a concentration of power
in a single person. Good citizens, even loyal members of Caesar's own Populare party, began to say
that he had become a danger to the Roman state and
wanted to be king. His rule, people feared, might
degenerate into outright tyranny—despotism.

Caesar himself contributed to the growing discontent by refusing to make his own position clear.
It appeared on the one hand that he was determined
to make himself king, and perhaps to claim divinity
as well. On the other hand he continued to insist
that he was a passionate believer in the old repub-
lican tradition with its faith in freedom and democracy.

Certainly he gave indications that the idea of becoming king was tempting him. For instance, he
appeared publicly in the regalia of the old Roman

kings once or twice, and even talked about moving
the capital to some such kingly city as Alexandria
or Troy. He set up a golden throne for himself in
the Senate, and had a statue of himself made and
placed next to those of the seven ancient Roman
kings. One person who was constantly urging him
to make himself king was Mark Antony.

Contrariwise, he was usually testy and annoyed
when citizens tried to treat him like a king or
greeted him with regal honors. He called out loudly
on one occasion, "My name is not king, but Caesar!"

One curious fact is that he made no formal, public effort to arrange for an orderly succession to his
regime in case anything should happen to him. Perhaps he had not made up his mind what to do.

At about this time Caesar began to be greatly
preoccupied with thoughts of death. His attitude
was fatalistic. When his friends urged him to guard
himself better, in order to lessen the danger of assassination, he replied calmly, "It's better to die
once than always be afraid of death."

Meantime, he set about making the best possible
and most vigorous use of his extraordinary powers.
Beginning in 45 B.C. he rocked Rome with an un-
ending series of laws and decrees. Some of his reforms were magnificently practical as well as far-
sighted. In a few short months he proved himself

to be one of the most enlightened and constructive rulers who ever lived.

One specific project dear to Caesar's heart was the rebuilding of Carthage and Corinth, the great cities in Africa and Greece which had been destroyed by Rome a century before. He knew that the world needed commerce and expanding trade, and that to have flourishing new towns across the seas instead of heaps of ruins would be very much to everyone's advantage.

Italy was becoming overcrowded, and he thought it would help matters if Rome were spread out. So he worked out a plan to found Roman colonies along the French Riviera, on the coasts of the Black Sea, in Spain, and elsewhere. Flourishing communities were thus built which preserved a healthy identity

for centuries. Many towns in France, Spain, and the Middle East are still "Roman."

Also he gave citizenship, which was a great privilege, to new residents of the empire. He passed a decree whereby anybody in Rome who was a qualified doctor of medicine or teacher of art or literature became a citizen. He wanted to encourage and reward brains.

He lowered tariffs, and reduced the burden of debt on people who owed money. He wrote a new labor code, reformed the currency system, encouraged agriculture, worked out plans for an adequate census, modernized the procedure whereby people had the right to vote, punished wealthy grafters and racketeers, and wrote new and better laws for selecting magistrates. He reformed the tax structure, and made a start toward codifying the whole body of Roman law.

Sternly he set himself against waste and excessive luxury. Extravagant spending was frowned upon. He clamped down on the use of litters to carry rich men through the streets, and even limited the amount of jewelry women could wear in public. Laws were passed cutting down the number of courses that could be served at a meal, even in private homes.

Then he inaugurated what we would call today a

vast public works program. He set out to rebuild
the unsatisfactory harbor at Ostia, the seaport of
Rome, and even to straighten the Tiber and make
it more navigable. He had projects for building new
amphitheaters and libraries, improving the system
of aqueducts, and opening canals. He even gave his
close attention to such items as sewage disposal,
street cleaning, and traffic control. Rome badly
needed reform in these matters. He worked out a
project for slum clearance, and planned to drain the
marshes nearby in order to prevent outbreaks of
malaria.

Politically his activity never stopped. He gave
clemency to most of his enemies, and astonished the
old Senators by his mildness and magnanimous behavior. Gratefully the citizenry erected a new temple called "The Temple of Clemency" to commemo-
rate his rule of mercy.

But also he moved to check political activity
against him. He closed up all the political clubs
where young hotheads gathered, and, to modify the
power of the Senate, increased its membership to
900 men.

He gave attention to other matters as well. Rome
had a growing, influential Jewish community at this
time. Caesar had always been strongly pro-Jewish,
and now he gave freedom of worship to the Jews.

He thought that the Jews were an important enliv-
ening influence on a city, and he wanted them to
retain their special identity.

In his spare time—and he always managed to
arrange his day so that he would have opportunity
to think—he amused himself by dictating an account
of the civil war.

Then he did something else of great interest: he
reformed the calendar. The old Roman calendar
had become unmanageable. It was based on the
moon, but the lunar month of 28 days was not a
satisfactory way to measure time. At the end of
every year there were always some days left over
that did not fit into any month, since twelve months
of 28 days each made a year of only 336 days, instead of 365. Thus the calendar was always lagging
behind. Caesar appointed a commission of astron-
omers to work out a reform, and as a result a year
of 365 days, beginning on January 1, and with a
leap year every fourth year, was set up. We still
use this calendar, and it is still called the Julian calendar in Caesar's honor. Also the month called July
was named for him.

While all this was going on Caesar, relaxing a bit,
decided to invite Cleopatra to Rome for a visit. On
her side, the Queen of Egypt was eager to have a

glimpse of Rome. She arrived in due course, and Caesar gave her a sumptuous public welcome. But then he was so busy and preoccupied with state affairs that he had little time for her.

❦ XVIII ❦

The Ides of March

Nobody knows exactly the origin of the fatal conspiracy against Caesar. There were probably several
different plots. The ringleader in the conspiracy that
succeeded was the lean, wiry Caius Cassius, an old-
time political leader and army officer. Even as a
youth Cassius had been known for his evil temper,
sourness, and jealousy of people more successful
than himself.

Cassius began to sound out other eminent Romans,
asking them to join him in a plot to murder Caesar.
(Tyrannicide—the killing of a despotic ruler for patriotic reasons—was not, it should be remembered,
considered to be a true crime in the Rome of those
days.) Several citizens joined Cassius, and the plot
got under way. One conspirator was Trebonius, an
old comrade-at-arms who was jealous of Caesar. An-

other was Decimus Brutus, who for years had been one of Caesar's closest friends and his foremost naval officer.

But Cassius could get nowhere with his plot if he did not bring another Brutus—Marcus Brutus—into it. He needed Brutus because of Brutus's great reputation as an honorable man. Brutus had towering prestige. He and Cassius were closely associated in their daily work, because Caesar had made them both praetors. Also they were brothers-in-law, for Cassius had married Junia, Brutus's sister.

Marcus Brutus was a complex person. It was always hard for him to make up his mind, and no matter what he did his conscience troubled him. He was pure in heart, but weak of will. As Shakespeare says, he was "with himself at war."

His wife, Portia, was a splendid woman. She had all the Roman virtues, including dutifulness and courage, and was brilliant and beautiful as well. Brutus did not confide in her that Cassius had approached him about murdering Caesar. She knew, however, that something terrible was preying on her husband's mind, because he could not sleep. So, one night when she was alone, she picked up a knife and stabbed herself deep in the thigh. She said nothing, and never once gave out a moan or cry of pain. Brutus discovered the next morning what she had done, and was horrified. Then she told him that, if she could inflict such pain on herself without whispering a word, surely he could trust her with whatever secret was troubling *him*. So he told her about the plot, and how whether to join it or not was tormenting him.

Caesar had high regard and affection for Brutus, ever if he was often muddle-headed. As has already been told, Caesar had been close to him for years, and freely forgave him for having joined Pompey at Pharsalus. Then, on returning to Rome, Caesar gave Brutus an important post, the governorship of Cis-alpine Gaul. Brutus had a considerable influence on him, and some people even thought that Caesar planned to make Brutus his eventual successor.

As to Cassius, Caesar had little regard for him, although he had made him a praetor. He no longer trusted Cassius. Shakespeare's passage about this is famous. He has Caesar say,

> *Let me have men about me that are fat,*
> *Sleek-headed men, and such as sleep o' nights:*
> *Yond Cassius has a lean and hungry look,*
> *He thinks too much: such men are dangerous.*

Caesar was pushing ahead with his reforms. He was full of new ideas for useful projects. But by this time his manner was becoming more dictatorial, and this offended people. He was high-handed with his old associates, and would tolerate no opposition. He did things which seemed to indicate that he held the old constitutional principles in contempt. Once he insulted the Senate gravely by addressing the Senators sitting down (as if he were on a throne) instead of standing, as was the custom.

On the other hand, when flatterers urged him to accept new honors, he rebuked them by saying that his honors "had more need to be cut off than extended." One night at home he had a violent emotional reaction after having heard widespread criticism of his policies. He tore off his shirt, bared his neck to friends who were present, and offered to let any man there cut it if he thought that he, Caesar, had exceeded his powers or was doing anything wrong.

In February, 44 B.C., he was appointed Dictator for life. No Roman had ever been given such a position before. It meant that Caesar was now permanent ruler of Rome and could never be removed from office except by assassination. Hence his enemies were reinforced in their determination to kill him for both selfish and "patriotic" reasons.

Caesar decided to go to far-off Parthia. His work in Rome was far from finished, but he could not overcome his yearning for more travel and conquest. He wanted to be back in the saddle again, leading his hard-bitten legions to new victories in new and glorious wars. Besides, it was important to make the eastern frontiers secure.

Caesar planned to be absent from Rome for two years, and to return through eastern Europe. He wanted to extend Roman rule to the Danube, and to fix this river as Rome's northeastern frontier.

Caesar announced that he would leave Rome for Parthia on March 19. So the conspirators had to hurry and make definite plans.

Caesar knew quite well that something unpleasant was in the wind. He had spies everywhere. What is more, all the omens were bad. A soothsayer openly predicted that he would be killed. Nevertheless, with magnificent boldness (or perhaps foolhardiness is a better word) he refused to take precautions. Indeed, he did the exact opposite, and even went so far as to defy fate by dismissing his faithful bodyguard. Either he still trusted his destiny, his star, without question, or he was deliberately courting death.

He continued to behave more regally, but at the same time refused to take any overt step toward becoming king. Mark Antony, on the occasion of a big feast and chariot race, three times tried to put a

crown on his head. Each time he refused to wear
it. But, soon after this, several citizens publicly
saluted Caesar as king. The tribunes had them
thrown into jail, thinking that this would be Caesar's
wish. But Caesar, furious, astonished everybody by
dismissing the tribunes from their posts.

Obviously, he still had not made up his mind, and
was torn two ways. So the public did not know what
to think.

At last Cassius won Brutus over to joining the mur-
der plot. Brutus sadly decided that he had no other
choice, and that it was his duty to do away with
Caesar in order to save the republic. So Cassius,
Brutus, and the others perfected their arrangements.
Caesar was scheduled to attend a meeting of the
Senate on March 15, the Ides of March, and the
conspirators determined to strike on this day.

On the 14th Caesar went to a dinner party at the
house of an old friend, Marcus Lepidus. There was
much good talk. Some historians say that Cleopatra
was present, but this is uncertain. Caesar was gay,
benevolent, and full of wisdom and banter. But also
he was preoccupied and busy with affairs of state,
even while at dinner. He was scribbling some notes
when he overheard a snatch of conversation. Somebody happened to be asking someone else what, if
death had to come, was the best way for a person

to die. Caesar's voice darted across the room: "The best death is always sudden."

That night Caesar's wife, Calpurnia, had evil dreams, one of which predicted her husband's death. Moreover an uncanny kind of storm suddenly began to rage in the heavens. Calpurnia could not sleep. The next morning she was so upset that she pleaded with Caesar not to go to the Senate. To please her, he agreed to postpone the session. The conspirators got word of this delay, which might frustrate all their plans. So they sent Decimus Brutus to argue with Caesar and get him to change his mind. The scheme worked, and thus Calpurnia's effort to save her husband failed.

Caesar, surrounded by a crowd of friends and courtiers, including Brutus and Cassius, then set out for the Senate. En route a soothsayer appeared. Shakespeare describes the scene thus:

CAESAR: Who is it in the press that calls on me?
I hear a tongue shriller than all the music
Cry "Caesar." Speak; Caesar is turn'd to hear.
SOOTHSAYER: Beware the Ides of March.
CAESAR: What man is that?
BRUTUS: A soothsayer bids you beware the Ides of March.

CASSIUS:	Set him before me, let me see his face.
CAESAR:	Fellow, come from the throng, look upon Caesar.
CAESAR:	What say'st thou to me now? speak once again.
SOOTHSAYER:	Beware the Ides of March.
CAESAR:	He is a dreamer, let us leave him: pass.

Even now, Caesar's life might still have been saved. He reached the Senate. A Greek named Artemidorus, one of Brutus's friends, had knowledge of the assassination plot. He wrote out a warning, and thrust this into Caesar's hand. But there was such a crush of people around Caesar that he never got a chance to read it. Also, the conspirators pushed Artemidorus aside, to get in first with other petitions and thus occupy Caesar's attention. As for Caesar, even though he was suspicious of some people, he still thought that the men surrounding him and clamoring for attention were loyal to him.

In the Senate hall, Caesar saw the soothsayer again. Caesar said dryly, "The Ides of March are come." The soothsayer replied, "Ay, Caesar, but not gone."

Then, at a signal given by one of the conspirators, when all of them stood close around Caesar, a henchman of Cassius named Casca struck the first blow. He stabbed Caesar in the neck, from behind, with

a dagger he had concealed in his robe. Caesar turned around in astonishment, exclaiming, "Why! This is violence!" He spat angrily at Casca and cried, "Vile traitor!" Then, since he had no other weapon, he struck back at him with his stylus, or pen, stabbing him in the shoulder.

All the other plotters now fell on Caesar. He tried to resist for a time, as they slashed at him with their daggers. Sharp blows rained down on him, but he still struggled. Then he saw Brutus approach, dagger in hand. Brutus struck him low in the stomach. Caesar murmured, "What! You, too, Brutus?" Then, with complete poise and dignity, he gave up resistance. He let his toga fall below his knees, so that his posture would not be undignified, and covered his head with another part of his garment, so that nobody could see the suffering in his face. Pierced by twenty-three wounds, he fell down at the foot of a statue of Pompey which he himself had caused to be put there. So Julius Caesar died.

❦ XIX ❦

Aftermath

After Caesar's death events moved swiftly. What happened has been famous in song and story ever since.

Although their grim task had been fulfilled, the conspirators were bewildered and confused. They had no plan for concerted action. Caesar's mangled body was brought back to his home by three of his slaves, and the populace, far from rising to the side of the murderers, remained inert—stunned with shock. Great Caesar gone! It was too much to believe.

Brutus made two colossal mistakes, one just before the murder, one after. First, he decided not to assassinate Mark Antony, Caesar's first deputy, together with Caesar. Cassius had felt that, if only as a matter of prudence, Mark Antony should certainly be killed too. But Brutus, clinging to his "idealistic" thoughts, overruled him. Brutus did not want the conspiracy to become a vulgar orgy of murder. Second, Brutus decided—once more against Cassius' will—to give Caesar a public funeral and to let Mark Antony speak.

Antony was, in Shakespeare's words, "a shrewd contriver." At first he was tempted to make a bargain of some kind with the killers. He even went so far as to have dinner with Cassius the night after the assassination, and suggested that Cassius take over the governorship of a province while he, Antony, stayed in power in Rome. But Cassius rejected the proposal.

Calpurnia was desperate with grief. She turned to Antony for sympathy and support, and they took stock of the situation. They had to move fast. If any movement against the murderers was organized, money would be needed. Calpurnia gave Antony all the money she could find in the house. The rest of Caesar's huge fortune was deposited elsewhere.

Antony then went to call on Cleopatra, who was distraught with shock. She was not popular in Rome, and for safety's sake Antony suggested that she return to Egypt at once. He promised to help her in any way he could.

The upshot of a confused period of uncertainty

and sorrow was the decision that Antony should set himself against the murderers, punish them if possible, and seize power in Caesar's name. Marcus Lepidus, who was in charge of security arrangements within the city, agreed to help him.

Then came the great speeches at Caesar's funeral. Brutus tried to justify the murder and appease the citizenry with calm words. Then Antony spoke and, as everybody who has read Shakespeare knows, his marvelous eloquence won the mob, inflamed it, and turned it ferociously against Brutus, Cassius, and their company.

Antony's oration, the one which begins, "Friends, Romans, countrymen, lend me your ears," was probably the most famous single speech ever made in ancient times. The enraged crowds, listening to his passionate words and hearing that Caesar had bequeathed part of his fortune to the citizens of Rome, spilled out into the streets, burning houses right and left and killing anybody who was suspected of having anything to do with the murder plot.

The conspirators were forced to flee. They went to Greece, and soon it became clear that they had accomplished nothing by killing Caesar. They did not save the republic but, on the contrary, wrecked it.

Octavius, Caesar's youthful grandnephew, was named in Caesar's will as his heir. He returned forthwith to Rome from an overseas post, where he had been studying, and joined with Antony and Lepidus to set up joint rule. The three consolidated their position in Rome, and made plans to catch and punish the conspirators.

The dramatic events that come thereafter are not part of our story, but we will summarize them briefly. Brutus and Cassius were beaten by Antony and Octavius in a complex double battle at Philippi, two years later, and paid for their murder of Caesar with death. Portia, Brutus's wife and a true daughter of the old Cato, killed herself by stuffing live coals into her mouth.

Later Antony went on to Egypt, where he too fell victim to the subtle wiles of Cleopatra. The triumvirate of Antony, Octavius, and Lepidus broke up in time, and Antony and Octavius became bitter enemies. Octavius defeated Antony in a decisive battle at Actium in 31 B.C., and Antony and Cleopatra committed suicide. Cleopatra, famous even in her manner of dying, had herself bitten by a poisonous asp.

Octavius, alone in the field after Antony's death, became the first Emperor of Rome, and assumed the name Augustus Caesar. So a new era in the long, magnificent, and disorderly history of Rome began. Some of the God-Emperors who followed Augustus

were splendid men; some were monsters—madmen. In the end Rome collapsed, and the Gauls whom Caesar had vanquished picked over its bare bones.

In summary, it may be said against Caesar that he put into play the forces that eventually killed the Roman republic. Nothing was the same after he crossed the Rubicon. Nevertheless, his accomplishment was great. In fact, his achievements as soldier and statesman are both colossal, and it was not his fault that the empire went to pieces later.

Caesar organized the entire known world of Europe, the Mediterranean, and the Middle East into a single unit, and sought to give it order, prosperity, and peace. The civilization inspired by Rome lived on, and still lives on, everywhere in Europe and the western democratic world today, even though Rome itself fell to the barbarians. And think what Caesar might have done if he had lived a little longer!

His dream was to give stability to the whole of the human race within the frontiers of civilization, and to see to it that it was ruled wisely, with dignity, decency and benevolence. Two thousand years later, the work he did still bears fruit.

Bibliography

Aside from Plutarch, Seutonius, and Caesar's own commentaries, which are the indispensable basic sources for any treatment of Caesar, I have found pleasure and profit in the following:

Barrow, R. H., *The Romans*, London, 1949.

Buchan, John, *Julius Caesar*, London, 1932.

Cary, M., *A History of Rome*, London, 1957.

Duggan, Alfred, *Julius Caesar*, New York, 1955.

Duggan, Alfred, *Three's Company*, London, 1958.

Frank, Tenney, *Life and Literature in the Roman Republic*, Los Angeles, 1956.

Grose-Hodge, Humphrey, *Roman Panorama*, Cambridge, 1949.

Hadas, Moses, *A History of Rome*, Garden City, N. Y., 1956.

Komroff, Manuel, *Julius Caesar*, New York, 1955.

Lempriere, J., *Classical Dictionary*, London, 1951.

Mills, Dorothy, *The Book of the Ancient Romans,* New
    York, 1937.
Warner, Rex, *The Young Caesar,* Boston, 1958.
Wilder, Thornton, *The Ides of March,* New York, 1948.

Also the *Encyclopaedia Britannica* has been useful, as
have been Shakespeare, Shaw, H. G. Wells, Breasted,
Toynbee, Langer, Durant, articles in the *Times* (London) and the New York *Times,* and, finally, the old German historian Mommsen.

Index

Achillas, 132, 134-35
Actium, battle of, 172
Adriatic, 74, 124
  blockaded by Pompey, 125
Aduatuci, 87
Aediles, 43, 57
Aegean Sea, 3
Africa, Caesar's campaign in, 140-43
  Optimate resistance to Caesar in, 140
Alexandria, 131-32, 151
  destruction of library in, 135
Alexia, 104-05
Alps, crossed by Caesar, 85
Ambiorix, Mark, 107, 114, 117, 151
  at Actium, 172
  Caesar offered crown by, 162, 164
  as Caesar's Master of the Horse, 132
  and Cassius, Caius, 170
  and Cleopatra, 170, 172
  in Egypt, 172
  oration at Caesar's funeral, 171
  personality of, 90
  at Philippi, 172
  suicide by, 172
Appian Way, 48, 57
Ariovistus, 86
Artemidorus, 166
Asia Minor, 13, 34-36
Augustus Caesar (Octavius), 17, 24, 145, 171-72
Aurelia (mother of Caesar), 16, 23, 39, 42, 64, 111
Avernians, 103-04

Belgae, 86
Bibulus, 74
Bithynia, 35
Britain, Caesar's forays into, 95-96
Brittany, 87, 111
Brutus, Decimus, 100, 122, 159, 165
Brutus, Marcus, 62, 128, 159-160, 164, 169-71
  Caesar stabbed by, 168
  death of, 172

Caesar, Gaius Julius, Aduatuci conquered by, 87
  as aedile, 57
  African campaign by, 140-43
  Ambiorix vanquished by, 102
  ambition of, 8, 110
  Antony, Mark, as friend of, 90, 114, 117, 132, 151
  appearance of, 25-26
  Ariovistus defeated by, 86
  assassination of, 15, 166-68
    aftermath of, 169-74
  athletic ability of, 24-25
  aunt of, 20, 42, 51
  austerity of, 108
  Belgae forced back by, 86
  birth of, 15
  book by, on Gallic campaigns, 83-84
  boyhood of, 23-24
  Britain invaded by, 95-96
  and Brutus, Decimus, 100, 122, 159, 165
  and Brutus, Marcus, 62, 128, 159-60, 164, 168

Caesar, Gaius Julius (*continued*)
building projects of, 152, 154-55
calendar reformed by, 156
and Cassius, Caius, 158-60, 164-65
and Cassius, Lucius, surrender by, 137
and Catiline conspiracy, 61, 62
Cato the Younger as enemy of, 58, 62, 72, 92, 114, 140, 143
character traits of, 8, 26, 107-108
and Cicero, 59, 62, 113
in Cisalpine Gaul, 56, 79, 85
in civil war with Pompey, 121-28
clemency shown to enemies of, 155
and Cleopatra, 130, 134, 136, 156-57
cleverness of, 110
Clodius as friend of, 59, 63-65, 112-13
in College of Pontiffs, 39-40
common sense of, 97
conspiracy against, 158-60, 162, 164-66
as consul, 68, 70-72, 74, 121, 147
courage of, 8
and Crassus, 47-50, 61, 65, 70, 74, 89-90
crown refused by, 162, 164
daughter of, 28, 42, 71, 111, 147
as dictator, 50, 121, 147, 161
in East, 34-36, 38
education of, 24
efficiency of, 110
in Egypt, 130-36

enlightened rule of, 151-52, 154-55
family background of, 10, 12, 15-22
father of, 16, 23, 27
in first battle, 35
in First Triumvirate, 70-71, 74, 89
first wife of, 27
at forty, 62
at forty-five, 74
fourth wife of, 72, 112, 165, 170
funeral of, 170-71
Gallic campaigns by, 77, 79, 83, 86-88, 93-95, 98-106
gentlemanliness of, 107
German armistice violated by, 91-92
Germans fought by, 86, 94
golden throne set up for, 151
as governor of Spain, 65-66
health of, 25
height of, 25
Helvetii defeated by, 86
Imperator title of, permanent, 150
indebtedness of, 49-50, 57, 65
and Labienus, Titus, 59, 100, 110, 144
lawsuit against Dolabella, 36, 38
in march on Rome, 114-15
and Marius, 21-22, 26, 28, 30, 51
as master of Mediterranean world, 145
mistrust inspired by, 110, 147, 150
morale in army built up by, 98
mother of, 16, 23, 39, 42, 64, 111

Caesar, Gaius Julius (*continued*)
Nervii destroyed by, 87
Nicomedes as friend of, 36, 38
Oak Leaf Crown awarded to, 35
as patrician, 21
as people's man, 22, 30, 50
in Pharsalus victory, 126-28
and pirates, capture by, 4-5
crucifixion of, 8
ransom paid to, 6
threat to, 5-6
and Pompey. *See* Pompey, and Caesar.
Pompey's secret papers destroyed by, 132
as Pontifex Maximus, 58-59, 147, 150
as Populare party leader, 57
Pothinus killed by, 135
as praetor, 62-63, 65
as Priest of Jupiter, 26
as pro-consul in Gaul, 74
pro-Jewish views of, 155-56
public funeral of, 170-71
as quaestor, 48-50
rationality of, 108
as realist, 108
reforms by, 151, 154-55, 160
Rhine crossed by, 92
in Rhodes, 3-4
Rubicon crossed by, 115, 117
ruthlessness of, 98
second wife of, 27-28, 30-31, 42, 51-52
Senate recording system set up by, 72
as Senator, 50
serious-mindedness of, 8
Servilia as friend of, 62
Shakespeare's view of, 107
Shaw's view of, 107
sisters of, 17, 58

at sixteen, 16, 26
as soldier, 9, 174
in Spain, 55-56, 65-66, 68, 122, 144-45
stamina of, 99
as statesman, 9, 122, 174
statue of, 151
and Sulla, 30-31, 33
as tactician, 83, 96
Tenth Legion as favorite of, 79, 82
third wife of, 52, 63-64
at thirty-four, 50
toga given to, 26
as tribune, 147
tribune dismissed by, 164
triumphs given in honor of, 146
at twenty-one, 33
Veneti subdued by, 87
"Veni, Vidi, Vici" message by, 137
and Vercingetorix, 103-05
versatility of, 108
wealth accumulated by, 65, 146
at Zela, battle of, 137
Calendar, reformed by Caesar, 156
Calpurnia, 72, 112, 165, 170
Carthage, 13, 16, 59, 152
Casca, 166, 168
Cassius, Caius, 158-60, 164-65, 169-71
death of, 172
Cassius, Lucius, 136-37
Catiline conspiracy, 61, 62
Cato the Younger, 58, 62, 72, 92, 114, 140
suicide by, 143
Cavalry, Caesar's, 82
Centurions, 82
Cicero, 59-60, 61, 72, 113
Cinna, 28, 30

Cisalpine Gaul, 24, 55, 74, 77-78
    Caesar in, 56, 79, 85
Cleopatra, and Antony, 170, 172
    appearance of, 131
    brother of, 130, 134-36
    and Caesar, 130, 134, 136, 156-57
    Egypt ruled by, 130
    invited to Rome, 156-57
    knowledge of, 131
    return to Egypt, 170
    Shakespeare's description of, 131
    suicide by, 172
Clodius, 59, 63-65
    death of, 112-13
Cohort, strength of, 79
College of Pontiffs, 39-40
Conquest of Gaul, The, 83
Consuls, 43-44
Corinth, 152
Cornelia, 27, 28, 30-31, 42, 51-52
Cossutia, 27
Cotta, 39
Crassus, and Caesar, 47-50, 60, 65, 70, 74, 89-90
    death of, 112
    in First Triumvirate, 70-71, 74, 89-91

Dolabella, 36, 38
Druids, 79
Dyrrhachium, 126

Egypt, 59
    Antony in, 172
    Caesar in, 130-32, 134-36
    intrigue in, 134
    money owed Rome by, 132
    Pompey assassinated in, 128
    war in, 135-36

Ethiopia, 136
Etruscans, 11-12

Feast of the Good Goddess, 63
First Triumvirate, 70-71, 74, 89, 111

Gaul, Cisalpine. *See* Cisalpine Gaul.
Gauls, 13, 21, 78-79, 122, 174
    Caesar's campaigns against, 77, 79, 83, 86-88, 93-95, 98-106
    as Caesar's cavalrymen, 82
Germans, 79, 86, 91
Gladiatorial games, 14
Gnipho, Antonius, 24
Greece, Caesar's campaign in, 124-28
    conspirators' flight to, 171
    Pompey's flight to, 122
Greek settlements, in southern Italy, 11

Hellespont, 136
Helvetii (Swiss), 79, 84-86

Ides of March, Caesar warned against, 165-66
Illyria, 74

Jerusalem, 67
Jews, Caesar's attitude toward, 155-56
Juba, King, 140, 142-43
Julia (aunt of Caesar), 20, 42, 51
Julia (daughter of Caesar), 28, 42, 71, 111, 147
Julian calendar, 156
Julian family, 15-17, 21, 51
Juno, 26
Jupiter, 26

Labienus, Titus, 59, 100, 110, 144
Latins, 11
Latium, 11
Legions, quality of, 46, 79
strength of, 79
Lepidus, Marcus, 164, 171-72
Lucca conference, 90

Marius, 19, 20-22, 26, 28, 30, 46, 51, 57
Mars, 12, 26
Master of the Horse, 45, 132
Mercury, 26
Metellus, 123
Miletus, 5-6
Military tribunes, 82-83
Mithridates, 35-36, 38, 137
Molo, Apollonius, 4, 38
Mucia, 68, 71
Munda, battle of, 144-45
Mytilene, 35

Nervii, 87, 99
Nicomedes, 35-36, 38
Numidians, 142-43

Oak Leaf Crown, 35
Octavia, 112
Octavius (Augustus Caesar), 17, 24, 145, 171-72
Optimates, 18, 28, 38, 68, 113
Ostia, 155

Parthia, 112, 161-62
Patricians, 17-18, 45
Pergamum, 6
Pharnaces, 137
Pharsalus, battle of, 126-28
Philippi, battle of, 172
Piso, 72, 94
Plebeians, 17-18
Po Valley, 13, 77, 88
Pompeia, 52, 63-65

Pompey, 66
appearance of, 68
Asiatic victories by, 67
assassination of, 128
and Caesar, 68, 71, 89-90, 111-14
civil war with, 121-28
as consul, 113
and Crassus, 70, 112
Crassus' widow married by, 112
at Dyrrhachium, 126
in First Triumvirate, 70-71, 74, 89
flight to Greece, 122
Julia married by, 71
at Lucca conference, 89-91
Mucia divorced by, 71
personality of, 68
in Pharsalus defeat, 126-28
pirates subdued by, 67
political affiliations of, 68
secret papers of, found at Pharsalus, 132
sons of, 144
triumphs given in honor of, 67
vanity of, 68, 90
Pontifex Maximus, 58-59, 147, 150
Pontus, 35, 38
Populares, 18, 30, 51, 57, 150
Portia, 159, 172
Pothinus, 134-35
Praetors, 43
Pro-consuls, 45
Pro-praetors, 45
Ptolemy XII, 130, 134-36
Punic Wars, 13, 59, 142

Quaestors, 43, 49-50

Ravenna, 78, 114
Remus, 11

Rhine River, 86, 92-93
Rhodes, 3, 38
Rhone River, 84-85
Romans, in Asia Minor, 34-35
  as builders, 14
  as citizens, 42
  as engineers, 14
Rome, army of, equipment of,
    79, 82
    organization of, 79
    political role of, 46
  Caesar's enlightened rule of,
    151-52, 154-55
  civil war in, between Caesar
    and Pompey, 121-24, 125-
    128
    between Marius and Sulla,
    30
  Cleopatra invited to, 156-57
  constitution of, 44-45
  corruption of, 18, 47
  democracy in, 44
  dictators of, 19, 30, 45, 113,
    161
  gladiatorial games in, 14
  leading families of, 10-11
  as monarchy, 12
  Octavius as first Emperor of,
    17, 172
  political system of, 14
  as republic, 12
  symbol of, 42
  triumphs held in, 67
  as world's greatest city, 10,
    14
Romulus, 11-12
Rubicon, crossed by Caesar,
    115, 117

Scipio, Africanus, 142
Scipio, Metellus, 140
Senate, 42, 155
  addressed by Caesar sitting
    down, 161

burned down by rioters, 113
Caesar honored by, 132
Caesar as member of, 50
golden throne in, for Caesar,
  151
recording system for proceed-
  ings of, 72
Senatus Populusque Romanus,
  42
Servilia, 62
Shakespeare, quoted, 107, 131,
  160, 165-66, 170-71
Spain, 14
Caesar in, 55-56, 65-66, 68,
  122, 144-45
Spartacus, 48
Sulla, 28, 30-31, 33, 36, 40, 42,
  44, 46, 51-52
Syria, 91, 112, 137

"Temple of Clemency," 155
Tenth Legion, 79, 82, 86
  mutiny of, 138-39
Thapsus, battle of, 143
Thessaly, 126, 132
Tiber, 11-12
Toga, manhood symbolized by,
  26
Transalpine Gaul, 74
Trebonius, 158
Tribunes, 43-44
Triumph, Roman, ceremonies
  of, 67
Triumvirate, First, 70-71, 74,
  89, 111

Veneti, 87
Venus, 12, 26
Vercingetorix, 103-05
Vesta, 27
Vestal Virgins, 27, 31, 33, 63

Zela, battle of, 137

LANDMARK BOOKS

1 **The Voyages of Christopher Columbus** by Armstrong Sperry
2 **The Landing of the Pilgrims** by James Daugherty
3 **Pocahontas and Captain John Smith** by Marie Lawson
4 **Paul Revere and the Minute Men** by Dorothy Canfield Fisher
5 **Our Independence and the Constitution** by Dorothy Canfield Fisher
6 **The California Gold Rush** by May McNeer
7 **The Pony Express** by Samuel Hopkins Adams
8 **Lee and Grant at Appomattox** by MacKinlay Kantor
9 **The Building of the First Transcontinental Railroad** by Adele Nathan
10 **The Wright Brothers** by Quentin Reynolds
11 **Prehistoric America** by Anne Terry White
12 **The Vikings** by Elizabeth Janeway
13 **The Santa Fe Trail** by Samuel Hopkins Adams
14 **The Story of the U. S. Marines** by George Hunt
15 **The Lewis and Clark Expedition** by Richard L. Neuberger
16 **The Monitor and the Merrimac** by Fletcher Pratt
17 **The Explorations of Père Marquette** by Jim Kjelgaard
18 **The Panama Canal** by Bob Considine
19 **The Pirate Lafitte and the Battle of New Orleans** by Robert Tallant
20 **Custer's Last Stand** by Quentin Reynolds
21 **Daniel Boone** by John Mason Brown
22 **Clipper Ship Days** by John Jennings
23 **Gettysburg** by MacKinlay Kantor
24 **The Louisiana Purchase** by Robert Tallant
25 **Wild Bill Hickok Tames the West** by Stewart H. Holbrook
26 **Betsy Ross and the Flag** by Jane Mayer
27 **The Conquest of the North and South Poles** by Russell Owen
28 **Ben Franklin of Old Philadelphia** by Margaret Cousins
29 **Trappers and Traders of the Far West** by James Daugherty
30 **Mr. Bell Invents the Telephone** by Katherine B. Shippen
31 **The Barbary Pirates** by C. S. Forester
32 **Sam Houston, The Tallest Texan** by William Johnson
33 **The Winter at Valley Forge** by Van Wyck Mason
34 **The Erie Canal** by Samuel Hopkins Adams
35 **Thirty Seconds Over Tokyo** by Ted Lawson and Bob Considine
36 **Thomas Jefferson** by Vincent Sheean

37 **The Coming of the Mormons** by Jim Kjelgaard
38 **George Washington Carver** by Anne Terry White
39 **John Paul Jones** by Armstrong Sperry
40 **The First Overland Mail** by Robert Pinkerton
41 **Teddy Roosevelt and the Rough Riders** by Henry Castor
42 **To California by Covered Wagon** by George R. Stewart
43 **Peter Stuyvesant of Old New York** by Anna and Russel Crouse
44 **Lincoln and Douglas** by Regina Z. Kelly
45 **Robert Fulton and the Steamboat** by Ralph Nading Hill
46 **The F.B.I.** by Quentin Reynolds
47 **Dolly Madison** by Jane Mayer
48 **John James Audubon** by Margaret and John Kieran
49 **Hawaii** by Oscar Lewis
50 **War Chief of the Seminoles** by May McNeer
51 **Old Ironsides, The Fighting Constitution** by Harry Hansen
52 **The Mississippi Bubble** by Thomas B. Costain
53 **Kit Carson and the Wild Frontier** by Ralph Moody
54 **Robert E. Lee and the Road of Honor** by Hodding Carter
55 **Guadalcanal Diary** by Richard Tregaskis
56 **Commodore Perry and the Opening of Japan** by Ferdinand Kuhn
57 **Davy Crockett** by Stewart H. Holbrook
58 **Clara Barton, Founder of the American Red Cross** by Helen Dore Boylston
59 **The Story of San Francisco** by Charlotte Jackson
60 **Up the Trail from Texas** by J. Frank Dobie
61 **Abe Lincoln: Log Cabin to White House** by Sterling North
62 **The Story of D-Day: June 6, 1944** by Bruce Bliven, Jr.
63 **Rogers' Rangers and the French and Indian War** by Bradford Smith
64 **The World's Greatest Showman: The Life of P. T. Barnum** by J. Bryan III
65 **Sequoyah: Leader of the Cherokees** by Alice Marriott
66 **Ethan Allen and the Green Mountain Boys** by Slater Brown
67 **Wyatt Earp: U. S. Marshal** by Stewart H. Holbrook
68 **The Early Days of Automobiles** by Elizabeth Janeway
69 **The Witchcraft of Salem Village** by Shirley Jackson

70 The West Point Story
by Colonel Red Reeder & Nardi Reeder Campion

71 George Washington: Frontier Colonel
by Sterling North

72 The Texas Rangers
by Will Henry

73 Buffalo Bill's Great Wild West Show
by Walter Havighurst

74 Evangeline and the Acadians
by Robert Tallant

75 The Story of the Secret Service
by Ferdinand Kuhn

76 Tippecanoe and Tyler, Too!
by Stanley Young

77 America's First World War
by Henry Castor

78 The Doctors Who Conquered Yellow
Fever by Ralph Nading Hill

79 Remember the Alamo!
by Robert Penn Warren

80 Andrew Carnegie and the Age of Steel
by Katherine B. Shippen

81 Geronimo: Wolf of the Warpath
by Ralph Moody

82 The Story of the Paratroops
by George Weller

83 The American Revolution
by Bruce Bliven, Jr.

84 The Story of the Naval Academy
by Felix Riesenberg, Jr.

85 Alexander Hamilton and Aaron Burr
by Anna Erskine Crouse and Russel Crouse

86 Stonewall Jackson
by Jonathan Daniels

87 The Battle for the Atlantic
by Jay Williams

88 The First Transatlantic Cable
by Adele Gutman Nathan

89 The Story of the Air Force
by Robert Loomis

90 Heroines of the Early West
by Nancy Wilson Ross

WORLD LANDMARK BOOKS

W-1 The First Men in the World
by Anne Terry White

W-2 Alexander the Great by John Gunther

W-3 Adventures and Discoveries of
Marco Polo by Richard J. Walsh

W-4 Joan of Arc by Nancy Wilson Ross

W-5 King Arthur and His Knights
by Mabel L. Robinson

W-6 Mary, Queen of Scots by Emily Hahn

W-7 Napoleon and the Battle of
Waterloo by Frances Winwar

W-8 Royal Canadian Mounted Police
by Richard L. Neuberger

W-9 The Man Who Changed China
by Pearl S. Buck

W-10 The Battle of Britain
by Quentin Reynolds

W-11 The Crusades by Anthony West

W-12 Genghis Khan and the Mongol
Horde by Harold Lamb

W-13 Queen Elizabeth and the Spanish
Armada by Frances Winwar

W-14 Simón Bolívar by Arnold Whitridge

W-15 The Slave Who Freed Haiti
by Katharine Scherman

W-16 The Story of Scotland Yard
by Laurence Thompson

W-17 The Life of Saint Patrick
by Quentin Reynolds

W-18 The Exploits of Xenophon
by Geoffrey Household

W-19 Captain Cook Explores the
South Seas by Armstrong Sperry

W-20 Marie Antoinette by Bernardine Kielty

W-21 Will Shakespeare and the
Globe Theater by Anne Terry White

W-22 The French Foreign Legion
by Wyatt Blassingame

W-23 Martin Luther by Harry Emerson Fosdick

W-24 The Hudson's Bay Company
by Richard Morenus

W-25 Balboa: Swordsman and
Conquistador by Felix Riesenberg, Jr.

W-26 The Magna Charta by James Daugherty

W-27 Leonardo da Vinci by Emily Hahn

W-28 General Brock and Niagara Falls
by Samuel Hopkins Adams

W-29 Catherine the Great
by Katharine Scherman

W-30 The Fall of Constantinople
by Bernardine Kielty

W-31 Ferdinand Magellan
by Seymour Gates Pond

W-32 Garibaldi: Father of Modern Italy
by Marcia Davenport

W-33 The Story of Albert Schweitzer
by Anita Daniel

W-34 The Marquis de Lafayette: Bright
Sword for Freedom by Hodding Carter

W-35 Famous Pirates of the New World
by A. B. C. Whipple

W-36 Exploring the Himalaya
by William O. Douglas

W-37 Queen Victoria by Noel Streatfeild

W-38 The Flight and Adventures of
Charles II by Charles Norman

W-39 Chief of the Cossacks
by Harold Lamb

W-40 Adventures of Ulysses
by Gerald Gottlieb

W-41 William the Conqueror
by Thomas B. Costain

j
92
G

3449

Gunther, John
Julius Caesar

EAU CLAIRE PUBLIC LIBRARY